A Seeker's Guide to Inner Peace: Notes to Self

I0429751

Trey Carland

The events in our lives serve as sign posts we can either choose to ignore or follow. If we ignore them, we might end up driving in circles for a while, in which case we will encounter recurring themes. If we pay attention and use our intuition as a guide, we might end up getting to our final destination in One Peace.

Published by Whitney Press

i

DEDICATION

I would like to dedicate this book to my loving wife Shelby, who has taught me more about life than anyone can imagine. Her love, strength and wisdom is truly inspiring.

Early Acclaim

"A Seeker's Guide to Inner Peace" is a spiritual gem. I love this well written and intelligent book. The light of love, compassion and wisdom shines through every page. Trey Carland writes in a personable and pragmatic manner that is both kind and wise. The reader is fully engaged and one senses that they could be sitting in the same room with the author enjoying an open and honest conversation with a true Heart friend.

The book is a journal of life situation encounters that reflect deep insights and realizations. They skillfully support the inner pathway to conscious freedom and inner peace. Throughout the book, Trey shares inspiring quotes, recommended books, helpful practices and meditations to meet those apparent obstacles the seeker meets. He then gently points toward the ever open doorway to the light that one genuinely is. The "Notes to Self" demonstrate a deeply contemplated life that is fully enriched by direct understanding. A Seeker's Guide is the seeker's choice."

~ Katie Davis,
Author of *"Awake Joy: The Essence of Enlightenment"*

Notes to Self

CONTENTS

Notes to Self

Introduction

There have been a number of great books written about enlightenment and self-realization, all of which point to the same simple idea that we are not confined individuals, but are connected on an intrinsic level that can not be denied. It is difficult to put into words, but there are so many beautiful ways to speak about it and pointers used to illustrate it. Most people tend to experiment with different teachings to see what works for them. Some people resonate with the more intellectual and philosophical discussions on what's true, while others like the more heart-centered focus, and others are drawn more toward the metaphysical realm for answers. Some prefer the study of religions and different philosophies, while others prefer the simple exploration of the essence of one's true nature. In my case, as with many others, I tried on many different flavors until I found one that fit.

Once my search for Truth began (see Chapter 1), I started reading books on all sorts of subjects (i.e. religion, mysticism, physics, cosmology, history, sociology, psychology, philosophy, you name it). Eventually, I discovered the simple pointers to Truth that shifted my attention to focus on the basic experience of being present. The words of Eckhart Tolle and Byron Katie resonated with me the most, but there are countless other spiritual teachers that have been extremely helpful in my search (see Teacher Resources section for a list). This book is my attempt to share those teachings, and my inspirations related to those teachings, with as many people as possible.

Once I discovered the fundamental teachings of enlightenment, non-duality, self-realization, etc., I realized that I couldn't just keep this to myself. I really didn't have a choice in the matter. This had to be shared with the world. I started giving away books and CDs by various teachers to anyone who showed the slightest interest. I became very enthusiastic about writing about my discoveries. As I encountered new teachings that resonated with me, I shared. As I read a powerful passage in a book, I shared. As I experienced a profound insight, I shared.

In the beginning, my sharing entailed sending messages to an email list I created of all of my friends and family. At one point a friend of mine, Lisa Zaslow, suggested that I start a blog. I didn't really know much about blogs at the time, but I did some research and eventually followed her advice.

Over the years I received enough positive feedback from readers to realize that people found it beneficial to follow along with my journey. I would occasionally receive feedback from someone who encountered something I had written at just the right time in his or her life to have a profound impact. A benefit was being felt by at least a few people, and that's all that really mattered to me.

When my friend, Lisa, later encouraged me to write a book, I told her that I really wanted to, but just didn't have the time. Years later, I realized that I had been writing a book all along, just one little piece at a time. In reality, it was writing itself through me, for me. For all intents and purposes, this is a book of notes to Self, from Self.

Now, as you read through the words contained here, it's being written by you, for you. These words wouldn't exist if it weren't for your awareness of them. You give them life just by looking at them. If you get an "Aha" from reading these words, or are touched in some way, or bitten by the "enlightenment bug" the way I was, then this book will have served its purpose. If you ever feel moved to share your own insights or reactions with the world, the blog from which this book was compiled is always available. This book is a living being, without an end, just as you are.

http://compassion-blog.blogspot.com

Chapter 1: In the Beginning

[A version of this article appeared in the April 2006 issue of *Spirit in the Smokies* magazine, published in Asheville, NC. It was originally titled, "From Epilepsy to Enlightenment." A copy of the original article is included in the Appendix.]

My life changed forever on November 7, 2004 when I had a grand mal seizure, totally out of the blue. For about a year prior to that I had been having what I affectionately called "revelation spells." These were brief moments that lasted about a minute or two where I felt like I was having some sort of divine revelation and everything suddenly made perfect sense. It was accompanied with a sense of euphoria and the loss of control over the thoughts that crossed my mind. It was as if my mind had a mind of its own and would wander off for a minute while I just watched.

I assumed that these uncontrolled thoughts were what led to the euphoric revelations, but I could never remember what my mind had thought of after the fact. While it was happening I could observe the thoughts and almost examine them, but I would quickly forget as they faded. All I could tell was that the thoughts seemed to be fairly mundane and random, but still seemed to contain an element of significance assuming they were indeed bringing about this feeling of revelation. It was a bit frustrating from that respect, but a pleasant feeling none the less. I was later told by a Neurologist that these were complex partial seizures.

After my first grand mal seizure, it was given a name – Epilepsy. This is a term given to anyone who has had more than one seizure, so it was not a diagnosis that helped answer any questions. In fact, none of the tests I had done answered my burning question of, "Why?" The only thing we were able to learn was that the seizures were originating from my left temporal lobe. There is surprisingly little known about epilepsy. In fact, about 70% of the cases have no known cause, which was frustrating but very compelling.

Those first few weeks were not very fun. Once the first grand mal hit, it opened the door for more to follow. I had to be put on medication fairly quickly in order to control the seizures, a fact to which I was quite resistant. I did not want to be dependent on a mind altering pharmaceutical for the rest of my life. I tried to wean myself off of what they put me on and had some more grand mal seizures. Since these are quite unpleasant, I reluctantly chose a drug with the least amount of side effects and stuck to it.

My wife and I began doing a great deal of research on the subject of epilepsy and came up with several possibilities from aspartame to mercury, none of which became the clear cause. As my frustration progressed and I adapted to the medication, I began seeking out alternatives. I began seeing an MD who was also an Oriental Medicine Doctor and started taking several herbal supplements and changing my diet. I also began seeing a counselor as a result of my moodiness (a possible side effect of my medication). I was very fortunate that my wife referred me to a counselor who helped me open my horizons of self awareness and turned me on to new ways of seeing things.

In reading about famous people in history with epilepsy, I began looking for commonalities. I heard about a possible link between epilepsy and shamans which compelled me to do some digging. The only thing I found at first was mention of some spiritual figures in history having epilepsy. So I began researching areas of religion and spirituality that I had not previously explored. I read an old comparative religion textbook I found in a box, which was interesting, but I found myself wanting to know more.

I saw a meditation class being offered at the Lotus Lodge and had a desire to attend, partly due to the Lotus Lodge being right near my home and partly because my curiosity had been piqued by what I had read about Buddhism. Meditation was a new and different experience that involved letting go of inhibitions and thoughts, while focusing on the breath. I experienced a "warm and tingly" feeling that left me wanting to know more.

I then became more eager to learn more about this area of the mind. I began reading books and web sites on quantum physics and spiritual and psychological aspects of life, each one illuminating more about myself and the world around me. I felt this strange desire to learn more about things of a spiritual and metaphysical nature, which was really something I had no prior interest in whatsoever. I was a little comforted and fascinated by this seemingly odd compulsion when I read a study linking the left temporal lobe of the brain to thoughts of a spiritual nature. It was dubbed the "God Spot" in the article, which studied meditating monks and praying nuns. So I figured there was at least a scientific explanation even if no one knew much else.

During this time of exploration, my wife and I began taking a shamanic dreaming class and enjoyed it greatly. One of our first homework assignments involved dreaming for someone else in the class who had a question they wanted answered. The results were stunning. Each of us actually had relevant information about the answer to a total stranger's burning question. Magically, this was at the same time I was reading David Hawkins' book. *Power vs. Force* (which my counselor recommended) which explained how we are all a part of a universal consciousness that we can tap into with kinesiology. I got to read about it and experience it first hand, thereby changing the way I viewed the world. It was then that I realized that I was given the gift of a life altering diagnosis in order for me to discover all that I was missing. These readings and experiences had changed my course from finding the cause and cure for my seizures to a search for enlightenment.

As for the seizures themselves, I have been reluctant to part with them. In fact, rather than continuing to up my medication until the seizures went away, which is what my doctors have been suggesting for the last year, I got them regulated so that I was no longer having grand mal seizures but continued to have "partials" about once a month or so. I felt like this was the only way to measure the impact of the alternative treatments I was trying. After all, how can you tell if you've gotten rid of them naturally if you get rid of them artificially?

However, the partial seizures have changed a bit since the pre-diagnosis days. I now experience an aura of anxiety as they set in rather than euphoria. I think this may be due to the fear that it might be a "big one," but I think there is something to learn from the experience itself. If I were able to experience the partials on a regular basis, without the concern of a grand mal, it would give me the opportunity to delve into them and possibly retain information on the seemingly random thoughts that occur. These strange "dreams" might hold some key to higher levels of awareness.

In the meantime, I am trying to lead a healthier life and practice mindfulness in everything I do. I have also been doing some non-dominant hand writing and drawing in an attempt to further explore portions of my brain I haven't used since I was young. I have also rekindled my desire to do what I can to make this world a better place through nonpolitical means. In short, I feel one step closer to where I never realized I needed to be, and I owe it all to something I never wanted to have, but now can't imagine being without.

Chapter 2: What Other People Think

August 11, 2005

We, as people, have a natural desire to please, because pleasing others brings us positive results. We also care about doing things that please us, but we learn, at an early age, that we can not always focus on pleasing ourselves and that pleasing others brings good things. To some extent, we learn what we should find pleasing when we are young, but we also have to figure out how to be pleasing to others. Therefore, we look to people whom we consider knowledgeable about these things for guidance, beginning with our parents. Through trial and error, we gradually figure out what they think is pleasing. As we age, we learn that we must please more and more people in order to get along in society (i.e. teachers, friends, ministers, bosses, etc.), which means we have to understand what more and more people find pleasing about us.

No matter how much we feel we do not care about what other people think of us, it is part of our core existence. Most of us have been raised in environments where we look to our parents to see how we should deal with the world around us. We look to our teachers and other role models to fill in the gaps that our parents do not fill. We look to our friends to see how we should deal with everyone else in order to be considered part of their peer group. We adopt different parts of each peer group's value system and end up with a collage of beliefs, aesthetics, and ideas about being pleasing to those who matter. The end result is how we interact with and interpret the world around us. This makes it hard to tell where we as individuals stop and where someone else begins.

For example, we do or don't do, say or don't say, think or don't think, hundreds of things during an average day based on how pleasing it might be for others. What does that say about us? Well, for one, we tend to try to judge ourselves through someone else's eyes. But, more importantly, we may not be doing what's best for us because we are too concerned about the opinions of others, thereby depriving ourselves of something that makes us happy.

If you are like me and feel as though you could really care less about what others think of you, try paying close attention to what you do and don't do during an average day. Ask yourself why you are doing the things you are doing. More importantly, when you find yourself tempted to do something that you decide against doing, ask yourself, "Why?" and look for the real reason. Do this frequently throughout the day and try to get in the habit of doing it regularly. By analyzing your own decision making process, you will likely find that a large number of your decisions stem from what you think others will think.

Most of your findings at first will be small and seemingly insignificant decisions involving what shirt to wear or where to eat lunch. However, you will likely be surprised at the number of things you prevent yourself from doing because of your fear of being looked down upon by others, even if they are not around. Pay attention to what you feel comfortable doing when no one is around versus things you would not do in their presence.

This may not seem to be earth shattering news since we all naturally need to function with other people and abide by certain societal customs that we can not completely ignore, but I think we are all much more caught up than we realize in what other people think. The real danger of this is that we cease to think for ourselves and rely on others to show us the way. In order to stop relying so heavily on those around us to know how we can be fulfilled, we have to focus on thinking for ourselves as much as possible. The problem is that it sounds much easier than it really is.

Chapter 3: A Personal Observation

October 29, 2005

I thought I would share an interesting observation I made about myself yesterday while rereading a paragraph in the book, *The Eye of the I*, by David Hawkins (this is the sequel to *Power vs. Force*). Due to losing my place a couple of times, I had to go back and reread the paragraphs a couple of times and did not think much of it until the third time. By then I had started seeing the similarity to what I was reading in my own life. To give you a little background, the book is about the path to enlightenment and is intended to bring about greater awareness in the reader. The section reads as follows:

> "Illumination refers to those spiritual states where sufficient barriers have been dropped, either deliberately or unconsciously, so that a greater context suddenly presents itself, and in so doing, illuminates, clarifies, and reveals an expanded field of consciousness actually experienced as inner light. This is the light of awareness, the radiance of the Self, which emanates as a profound lovingness. Although, for many people, the experience may not last (as in near-death experiences), the residual effect is permanent and transformative. In due time, the light is likely to return again for periods of infinite bliss, peace, and silence, followed by a profound gratitude for the gift."
>
> David Hawkins, *The Eye of the I* (page 30)

It goes on to say that most people who experience this become driven to obtain it again and go to great lengths to regain it. After reading it for the fourth time, I realized the similarity between what I used to refer to as "revelation spells" (a.k.a. partial seizures) to the concept of illumination referred to in the book. Then I realized that being diagnosed with epilepsy has been quite a transformative and life altering experience for me, and has driven me to read books I never would have read and to take classes I never would have taken (most of which have had some sort of psychological or spiritual connection). I have simply been attributing my growing interests in these areas as a determination to find the cause of my seizures. However, I think I have an ulterior motive that I was not aware of prior to rereading this section of the book, which is to find a way to tap into that feeling I get when I experience one of these revelation spells.

I thought it was interesting in several ways, so I thought I would pass it along to some of you who are involved in my growing spiritual awareness.

Chapter 4: Practicing Compassion

July 22, 2006

I wanted to share some ideas/insights with you that have been going on recently. A friend of mine recently challenged a lot of the people he knows to allow compassion into every moment of their day for several weeks straight. Being a person who has been doing a lot of soul searching of late, I took up the challenge. I did, however, add another component that my recent readings stressed as being important, which is to surrender positionality. The two seemed too congruent not to try both simultaneously.

I made myself several post-it notes and put them in places where I would see them on a regular basis and started trying to focus my attention as much as possible during each day. It basically involves learning how to relate and empathize with everyone and everything you come in to contact with on a daily basis, and realizing that we are all human beings trying to do what we feel is the best thing to do in any given situation. We are all products of our environment and upbringing and our actions will not always be what someone else would do. In other words, we can't help being the way we are.

All of our values and beliefs are based on our past experience as well. Since we don't always react well when those beliefs are challenged (i.e. we get defensive), it helps to recognize when we are reacting solely out of a defensive place based on our own structured beliefs, whether they are true or not. Plus, who's to say we've got it all figured out anyway? This also helps you realize that when other people react, they may be reacting from a defensive place as a learned reaction.

I'm currently reading The Art of Happiness by the Dalai Lama, and he has some very powerful things to say about compassion. The most notable quote so far is:

"Within all beings there is a seed of perfection. However, compassion is required to activate that seed which is inherent in our hearts and minds..."

The Dalai Lama
(http://www.happylifeu.com/DalaiLamaHappiness.html)

As for my personal observations on trying to allow compassion, it seems that there are many situations where I just don't know how to respond with compassion, or feel as though I am, but seem to receive information to the contrary. It seems like compassion (a vague term in itself) is not something we can just turn on, but a highly complex recontextualizing of stimulus and response behaviors.

In fact, it seems like I need examples to guide me such as "If you encounter a situation like this, a compassionate response would be something like this." Life is so complicated, you could likely fill volumes with this type of information, but I don't think everything you will ever encounter needs to be covered as you will eventually "get it" on your own after you start practicing and have the willingness to try in the first place.

In closing, I hope you all are doing well and that you may decide at some point to try your hand at this (keep me posted if you do). I think if everyone took this challenge (and it is a bit of a challenge), the world would be a better place.

Chapter 5: World Peace Starts at Home

August 25, 2006

As many of you know I have been doing a fair amount of research lately on life, consciousness, and things that might be considered more spiritual or metaphysical in nature (I've read that epilepsy does that to some people :-). What I have learned in the last year or so has just fascinated me enough to want to share it with others.

Since I come from an academic background, I have been approaching it all with some hesitation and skepticism, but have been pleasantly surprised at the consistency and coherence I am finding along the way (among scientific discoveries and a variety of spiritual philosophies). There obviously has not been such a major breakthrough wherein all of the skeptics are forced to agree (there is always a way to find a fault in something if you want to badly enough).

The conclusion I've come to so far is that it really doesn't matter if you believe what any of the major religions have said for hundreds of years. What does seem to be clear is that being a good person and taking responsibility for your actions leads to good things. Learning to be compassionate is a fundamental part of it all, no matter what your faith or scientific background, and will lead to happiness in your life if it's actively pursued. It also seems to be highly contagious, which could have far reaching implications.

The problem is that it's not easy to be kind and compassionate to everyone we know, especially if they are not kind to us. This is where certain ideas come into play to help us out. For example, the quotes below summarize a great deal without going into much detail, and can also serve as potential building blocks for structuring a happier more peaceful existence. There's a lot more information out there that supports these ideas, as well as specific tools for fostering happiness (not all of which are reliant on the common theme illustrated below).

Notes to Self

"Internal peace is an essential first step to achieving peace in the world. How do you cultivate it? It's very simple. In the first place by realizing clearly that all mankind is one, that human beings in every country are members of one and the same family."

The Dalai Lama
(http://www.care2.com/greenliving/dalai-lama-quotes-on-peace.html)

"Everything is an aspect of this infinite intelligence, every person, every animal, every tree, every star and every planet, and every micro-organism, however small, is ultimately an equal aspect of the very same energy. There is no separatedness except as an illusion created by the ego and five physical senses; we and the Universe without exception are one."

Adrian Cooper
Our Ultimate Reality: Life, The Universe and the Destiny of Mankind (page 88)

Chapter 6: Wake Up Calls

September 16, 2006

Thanks, in part, to my friend Jason's near fatal fall (he's healing well now by the way - thanks for the vibes), I have come to realize more fully something about myself that I think may be of use to others. Given that I don't believe in accidents and that everything we encounter has some significance, I think that major events in our lives are even more significant. We all periodically get shocking, and sometimes nearly fatal, messages in life that we refer to as wake up calls (my most recent wake up call was a grand mal seizure). I think these major events in our lives are designed to tell us something about the direction our life is going, more specifically that we may be pursuing the wrong path. Often times it seems like events have to be life altering to adequately get our attention, probably because we tend to bounce back too quickly from less dramatic wake up calls.

A lot of us have been lucky enough to survive life's wake up calls and find ourselves on a totally different and more beneficial path. One of the keys to a more positive outcome seems to be to look at these events from a different, more impartial perspective and pay close attention to what was going on when the event took place. There are clues everywhere guiding us in the direction we need to be going, but if we don't pay attention to the little things, it may take something more significant to get our attention focused where it needs to be. I'm very grateful for everything I've been through since it all has helped shape who I am today, and I like who I am today :-)

Chapter 7: The Power of Compassion

October 9, 2006

I wanted to share a story out of *The Lost Art of Compassion* by Lorne Ladner, that you might find inspiring. It is an actual case in point on using compassion to better your world, and it goes something like this (please note that I am paraphrasing here):

A student of Buddhism is at a dinner party with a group of intelligent and wealthy individuals. They had chatted a bit about Buddhism, but then conversation had turned to more daily life type things. One of the guys (John) told this story about how one night he heard a thud outside. He ran to the window to see that his neighbor had just backed into his BMW (parked on the street) and drove away and parked in his garage. John went down and saw that the damage was pretty extensive so he went over to the neighbor's house and began ringing the bell. No answer. He tried knocking for a while and eventually gave up.

His insurance company sued the neighbor and eventually won a $5,000 settlement for the damages. After he got the car repaired, he found one day that it had been deeply scratched all the way down one side. John suspected his neighbor, but didn't witness it so he had it fixed himself. After he got it painted, the same thing happened again. He felt sure his neighbor was to blame so he went over to confront him about it. The guy denied it and threatened to sue him for slander for accusing him of such. He gave up and had it fixed again.

At this point John was constantly peeking out the window in hopes of catching his neighbor in the act and it was driving him crazy. He asked the guests at dinner what they would do. Suggestions ranged from hidden cameras to sensitive alarms (he had to park in the street). The Buddhist student wondered what his teacher would suggest in that situation and instantly knew. He suggested that John should take a gift to his neighbor and apologize for the trouble he has caused him. The people at dinner thought that was crazy and pointed out that the neighbor was a low life.

However, John decided to do just that. He knew his neighbor was a golfer, so he went and bought very expensive golf balls (the type people would not ordinarily buy for themselves). He went to his neighbor's house who was wary to see him. He gave him the gift and apologized for accusing him of scratching his car and wanted to give him a token of apology.

A little while later, the neighbor showed up at John's door. It looked as if he had been crying. He thanked John profusely for the gift and said that no one had ever been so nice to him. The neighbor told him if he ever needed anything, just to let him know. From that point on, he was the best neighbor one could ask for.

Just a little food for thought that might benefit you in your lives. It could have saved me problems a few years ago when I was having problems with my neighbors. Maybe it can do the same for you in some way.

Chapter 8: A Few Tips on Life

October 12, 2006

For those of you who are interested in some basic tips on living the life you want to live, I have come up with a basic list from my own experience (and research) that might benefit you.

Pay attention to your thoughts as often as you can. The mind is always working on something and we are oblivious most of the time. However, what it's doing (or thinking) affects everything we do and say, so start keeping tabs on the thoughts going on in it. This is referred to as practicing mindfulness and it does take practice.

Break your routine. This includes what you would ordinarily say in response to something, as well as what you do in your daily activities. This also translates into "think before you speak or act."

See what thoughts occur as a result of changing your routine. If you are practicing mindfulness and choose to do or say something different (or nothing at all) from what you would ordinarily do or say, interesting thoughts or feelings may arise. Pay attention to those and ponder them.

Stop to smell the roses. When you are feeling trapped in your routine or stressed out about something, take a moment to stop and clear your mind of the habitual thoughts for a moment. Take a deep breath and look around at the scenery and find something to appreciate. Practicing gratitude is an important thing to do and can make you feel better about things, but it too takes practice.

Some people say that you don't own your thoughts, you just listen to them. Thoughts tend to be based on years of training and are not always the types of thoughts that have your own best interest at heart. So, no matter what you are interested in doing with your life, being mindful will be a key to making it happen. With practice, you can begin noticing when negative thoughts start to enter your head and intervene before they take you somewhere you don't want to be. Over time, you can maximize the number of positive things that happen in your life and minimize the negative things.

Chapter 9: Some Suggested Reading

October 24, 2006

I've been out of town for the last week at our conference in Reno (which is a nice town nestled in some beautiful mountains). Now I'm playing catch up and trying to recover from a cold that I caught on the way out there. In the meantime, I've run across so much information I wanted to share that I don't know where to begin, so I'll just jump right in.

Since my last update, I've added a new book to the group of books I'm currently reading, *A New Earth: Awakening to Your Life's Purpose* by Eckhart Tolle (author of The Power of Now: A Guide to Spiritual Enlightenment). It delves into what you find when you start paying attention to your thoughts and how they affect your life. I highly recommend this book, as well as the others I have mentioned previously (and look forward to reading others recommended to me by friends). I will probably be talking about it more in the future.

I also wanted to mention that the recent issue of *What Is Enlightenment* magazine has a two part interview with Brian Swimme (a mathematical cosmologist). Part one is entitled "Awakening to the Universe Story: Comprehensive Compassion" (see link below). Not long after I made the personal comparison between gravity and love, I found out that this idea was not new (not that I thought it was). Swimme says, "gravitational attraction is an early form of compassion or care." He talks a great deal about the importance that compassion has played in the evolution of the world. I felt quite encouraged by what I read in his interview as he has a lot of great ideas about the evolutionary track we are on (both past and future), so check it out if you're interested.

http://www.wie.org/j34/swimme1.asp

That's all for now. I hope all is well with you and yours. Keep me posted on your lives as well. I enjoy getting feedback from others, whether they are through the blog or sent directly to me. Enjoy the changing seasons and make the best of everyday.

Chapter 10: Yin and Yang

October 26, 2006

I rediscovered a poster I made almost 10 years ago when I was working on my second master's degree (I must be getting old ;-). I was in a counseling class where we had to bring in a collage that represented us and present it to the class.

I decided to cut out words that I printed off on a computer and taped them to a poster on which I had drawn a Yin Yang symbol (see table below for the words). I didn't have much knowledge of the Yin Yang and just knew that it represented a balance between feminine (Yin) and masculine (Yang) traits.

The words I chose were based on what I thought to be more masculine qualities vs. what I perceived to be more feminine traits. If I had it to do over again, who knows how it would look, but the gist is that I felt out of balance, having very few qualities on my feminine side.

Yin
Kindness
Nurture
Feel
Equality
Compassion
Goodwill
Help
Humble
Touch
Human
Empathy
Acceptance
Tranquility
Peace
Care

Gentle
Support
Harmony
Cultivate
Respect
Love
Natural

<u>Yang</u>
Truth
Open Minded
Analyze
Global
Logical
Imagine
Consistence
Reason
Reflect
Create
Generalize
Learn
Think
Introspection
Speculate
Vision
Rationalize
Cynicism
Justice
Wisdom
Skeptical
Educate
Theorize

Many years and life altering experiences later, I now feel more connected with my feminine side and am now even aspiring to tap into more of those traits. In fact, based on what I've read so far, if we could all open up to the Yin traits I listed and extrapolate them to apply to everyone and everything unconditionally, then we could find true happiness in everything we do and see. Just some added food for thought. Take care and be grateful for what you have.

Chapter 11: Regarding Mindfulness

October 30, 2006

Well, not long after my six month anniversary of being seizure free (meaning I could drive again for a few days) I had a partial seizure. Oh well, I'm apparently not quite ready to be free of them. Anyway, I wanted to share some other information that I had recently come across that I found quite powerful.

The first is a quote someone passed along by an author named Rosenburg (not an exact quote), "Behind every criticism, judgement, or blame resides an unexpressed or unfulfilled need or want." This reminds us to be present and aware of how you are feeling as often as possible. I am planning to read *Wherever You Go, There You Are: Mindfulness Meditation in Everyday Life* by Jon Kabat-Zinn to help increase my awareness of the present moment.

On a similar note, while trying to incubate a dream (a technique used in shamanic dreaming) on being granted the power of presence, I had some simple advice come to me: Think before you say something and don't let an unkind word out of your mouth.

Some ideas have come to me regarding mindfulness and not getting hung up in the future or past events. Everything you've done to this point was absolutely necessary to your survival. Look back for guidance but don't have regrets about it. Everything in the future will turn out just as it's supposed to, so don't waste energy with needless worry.

Also, I have been exposed to the concept of Ho'oponopono (an old form of Hawaiian healing that translates into "to make right" or "to rectify an error") from several places now and recently missed a local workshop on the subject. However, there is a great deal of information available on the internet about it.

Taking responsibility for all that happens and taking action when trouble spots arise are at the fundamental core of the practice (which brings us back to awareness). Here is some basic information on how it works:

Notes to Self

(taken from http://www.idreamcatcher.com/hooponopono)

"Cleaning is the actual Ho'oponopono practice. Cleaning what? You clean yourself from subconscious garbage – programs that run your life without your participation.

Ho'oponopono process is very simple. Actual Ho'oponopono cleaning process consists of repetitions of the following phrases:
* I Love You
* Please forgive me
* I am sorry
* Thank you

These phrases repeated will ignite the self transformation process for the practitioner."

Learning about the practice made me feel a bit better about dealing with my life (and not sweating the little things), so I wanted to share it with you as well. Keep me posted on your experiences as well.

Chapter 12: Anniversary Thoughts

November 7, 2006

Today is my two year anniversary. It was two years ago today (November 7, 2004) that I had my first grand mal seizure and was diagnosed with epilepsy. What an earth shattering event it was. A lot has changed since then and I am grateful for it all. In fact, I have learned to be more grateful for everything I have and everything I have been through as a result of this life altering event. I also think that it is no coincidence that it happened right around election time. At that time I was getting sucked deeper and deeper into the political wranglings of our country's leaders and losing sight of what's really important – leading a joyful life.

Now, I have grown to realize that no matter who controls what country, I can be a whole person and lead a fulfilling life. I can choose not to let external issues control my life and find inner peace if I look deep enough. I can even feel compassion toward those people who have lost hard fought elections, even if they happened to be less than honest while in office.

Ultimately, the only things that can affect us directly are those things that we allow to affect us. We have the power to decide how to respond to what happens in our daily lives and my personal recommendation would be to respond positively regardless of the situation. Be good to everyone even if they are not good to you and you can tap into something that the Dalai Lama refers to as the "seed of perfection in all of us."

Everything we do or think affects everyone in some way, whether it's directly or indirectly, so it's important to act in accordance with the highest good. Treating everyone with compassion and generosity, and being grateful for all we have is one of the best ways I know to proceed. I hope you will consider doing the same if you are not already.

It's a tall order I know, but one that I am trying to implement in my life. All thanks to a diagnosis that could have been an ongoing tragic event in my life if I had let it be. Instead, I can now say that developing epilepsy is one of the best things that's ever happened to me. So, take care of yourselves and be grateful for everything you have.

Chapter 13: Choose to Be in Control

November 21, 2006

I've been paying attention to my own thoughts a lot more lately (practicing mindfulness) and learning a great deal about myself in the process. A great deal of what I do is based on habit or trained response. It's like the brain is a computer programmed with a series of "if" "then" statements (if I do this, then it will bring about this result). This is basically the role of the ego.

The ego is a survival mechanism that helps us avoid injury as we develop. We innately try to avoid unpleasant things and instead bring about a pleasurable outcome. However, as we grow, so does the ego's role in running our lives, which can become very detrimental to our development and prevent us from finding true happiness. Many of the books I have read recently talk in great detail about the ego, but I won't delve too deeply here. I could probably write a book of examples from my life alone on things my ego led me to do that weren't in my best interest.

Now that I have become more aware, I have noticed that I have a tendency to always be doing something and allow certain things in my environment to run my life. This may be out of fear or a way to distract myself from dealing with something I'm not ready to deal with, but that's a discussion for another time. The bottom line here is that years of unconscious living has caused me to lose sight of the fact that I have the ability to choose what I do and how I respond to my external circumstances, regardless of what my ego has to say about it.

By the way, Thanksgiving is coming up and it's a great time to practice gratitude for all that you have. Gratitude is a wonderful thing so make sure you take time out to think about all of the things you have to be grateful for and feel free to share. Personally, I'm grateful for every single thing I've ever experienced, as well as every person I have had the pleasure to communicate with, because it has all had the cumulative effect of making me the person I am today. So thank you :-)

Chapter 14: Getting Involved

November 29, 2006

I hope your Thanksgiving was as good as ours. We went to Florida to visit Shelby's relatives that we don't get to see very often. In fact, she was able to reunite with her half-brother and half-sister whom she had not seen in almost 15 years (since the death of their father). It was a wonderful experience for everyone involved and I was glad to be there for it. Interestingly enough, the reunion was brought about by a dream Shelby's aunt Sonya had. Her aunt acted on the dream by reaching out to us all and helped make the reunion happen. The love was everywhere despite the anxiety leading up to it.

During conversations with Shelby's various family members, I learned things about everything from gardening techniques to remodeling tips to interpersonal relationships. The wealth of information learned on this trip is greatly appreciated. In fact, at the end of this note, I will share the tips related to fostering loving relationships since I feel this information is valuable to everyone who wants to have one.

One of the key pieces of information that I have learned previously, and have been trying to remember, is summed up by this quote, "When someone makes a statement, they are not asking you for something. If they are, they need to ask it." This seems simple enough, but I have found that I am in the habit of automatically jumping into action when someone makes a statement that implies they are in need of something. This gets you into trouble though, because it is based on an assumption, which is based on projection, which is based on past experience or programming. I have been focusing on not jumping in to fix things when a problem is stated and it seems to make life less complicated and more clear cut. If you find yourself doing the same thing, you might want to try refraining from assuming the role of fixer before someone asks for your help.

Shelby and I were discussing this and other things on the drive back from Florida and we stumbled on an issue with which I wanted to come to terms. How and when do you offer help to someone whom you think needs it, but who may not know they need help or even want it. Or, when do you get involved when you see something happening that you know does not need to happen and will have negative outcomes if it continues. A basic example of this is when you see a parent mistreating a child. You can see that the situation is a continuation of the same old cycle (i.e. parent mistreats child, child later becomes parent and mistreats his/her child, etc.) and yet it's not your place to intervene. Or is it? Do you ignore it if it doesn't directly affect you and just let the parties involved live the lives they were intended to lead? They have their life lessons to learn after all.

We were discussing this issue and not getting any clear resolution. There is an obvious problem in that the observer is assuming that he or she has a better solution to the situation. The degree of separation also has to be considered. It makes more sense to offer helpful suggestions to a family member in need than it does to a complete stranger. We kept going back and forth on this because I was looking for some rules of engagement to know when to get involved and none were clear cut.

We took a break from the conversation as we stopped for a quick bite to eat. While eating in the car, we realized that we had parked right next to a case of exactly what we were discussing. The man and woman next to us were arguing vehemently about something. She was very pregnant and standing in front of the car refusing to talk to him or even get back in the car. A young boy was in their back seat crying because of all the yelling, and an elderly woman was in the passenger seat sleeping (I'm not sure how). The man, after trying to tell the woman to get in the car because her son needed her, decided he would give her to the count of five to get in the car or he was leaving without her. At this point I wanted to do something, but had no idea what to do without knowing what they were fighting about.

Well, after counting to five he started to leave thinking she would give in. Of course she did not. He finally made good on his word and left. We just sat there and continued to eat, though I felt quite bad about it. After about 10 minutes she had sat down on a bench and cried a little. I finally went over and asked her if she was okay (unsure as to what to say). She smiled and said yes. I asked her if she was sure and she nodded. I said that I just had to make sure and I left.

We sat in the car for another minute before we hit the road again. I started second guessing what I should have said, but quickly realized that I had said exactly what I was supposed to say. We also discussed the fact that she was at a busy gas station with a phone inside if she needed to call someone. Though I was reassured by the fact that she would be okay, it was difficult for me to get it out of my mind.

The next day, on our second leg of the trip home, we parked at a rest area. While I was waiting for Shelby to return to the car, the woman parked next to us could not get her car started. She also could not get the hood up on her car after several attempts. This time I got out without an invitation to help and offered my services. I could tell she was a bit reluctant to accept help from a total stranger (which is a sad state of affairs in and of itself), but we were able to get the hood up. She smacked on the loose battery cable (as she had apparently done a number of times) and was able to get it started. She thanked me a couple of times and left. I felt good that I was able to help and was glad that nothing mechanical was wrong (I would have been unable to help beyond a jump start).

Thanks to these situational gifts, I decided that there is not a clear cut time and place to involve yourself in someone else's life. There is no magical list of criteria to check against before offering a helping hand to someone in need of direction or assistance. It's all shades of gray.

Oh well, maybe as I continue to grow I will develop a keener sense of when and how to get involved in another person's life. I can safely say that I am glad that Shelby's aunt Sonya got involved in our lives to help bring about a long overdue family reunion.

Notes to Self

List of Relationship Tips from Shelby's aunt Judith, whose husband, Cecil, has been battling terminal cancer for some time now.

- Always kiss hello and good bye
- Have a meeting night once a week to discuss things that are on your mind
- Go for walks where you talk about what you like/love about each other and what you like/love about yourself (you can't love someone else unless you love yourself)
- Don't allow yourself to act as your partner's parent
- Lead a full social life together
- Alternate decision days (one person gets to decide what to do/buy one day and vice versa)
- Each person pick a hobby that they want to do with their partner (i.e. one person picks dance lessons, the other person picks tennis lessons)
- If you can't say something nice, don't say anything at all
- Have a romantic date night once a month
- Don't be afraid to ask your partner for something you want

Chapter 15: Making Life More Joyful

December 12, 2006

I have compiled a list of attitudes that are revisited quite a bit in the literature about obtaining joy. I will try not to spend too much time on each item but still do them some justice.

Gratitude - Always be thankful for everything you have and have done. Spend some time each day just being grateful for everything you are. If you ever catch yourself revisiting a time when you did something foolish and getting embarrassed by it all over again (something I catch myself doing from time to time) forgive yourself and remember that everyone is doing what he or she thinks is right at that particular time in life. We can not fault ourselves for making mistakes, it comes with the territory and helps shape us into the wonderful people we are today. Be thankful and not regretful.

Openness - This is basically being open to all experiences and people without judgment. We are lightning quick to categorize people and experiences when we encounter them, so it seems difficult to catch much less rectify. However, it's important to realize that we are doing ourselves more harm than good by judging other people and events. They, too, are doing the best they know how at this given point in their lives and are prone to make mistakes just as we have in the past and will likely do so in the future. We also have to be careful not to judge ourselves, nor think about how others might be judging us based on what we do or say (it's a slippery slope).

Compassion - This is something that I have been "preaching" about for a while now and is very interrelated with being open. However, this goes a step beyond simply not judging someone to be an egomaniac. Compassion means caring about everyone regardless of their predispositions for annoying habits or poor behavior. Try to remember that we are all connected and share a common bond, and that we are all products of our environment. Realize that those who suffered most when they were young are often the ones who cause the most suffering when they are older. Try to be empathetic with their situation and show them what it's like to be kind as they may not have seen it first hand. You will be surprised at the effect this can have on a person.

Mindfulness - This involves paying attention to what you are thinking and what you are experiencing as much as possible. You really can't begin to make positive changes in your life without it. If you are just floating through life on your daily routine, and not paying attention to what you are doing, then your life will likely fly by without feeling very fulfilling. If you are truly happy by just following your routine, then please don't let this stop you. If you feel like something is lacking or that you could be happier or just want to experience true joy, then start paying attention and consider doing some basic meditation during the day. It may take a little practice to do at first, but it feels good to do and is a good exercise for living.

Present - Try to remain in the present moment as much as you can. We spend a great deal of our time worrying about an impending engagement or future obligation or goal, as well as reliving past events for further investigation. Once you start paying attention to your thoughts, you will realize that this is basically what we spend most of our time doing. We are well trained in that way by our daily routine. Try to stop and realize you're somewhere else in time. You can still be present while planning or working or making breakfast. If you can realize the past doesn't matter and realize that worrying about the future doesn't change it, you can realize the importance of being in the present moment. It, too, feels good to be in that place, though I still can not sustain it for long periods without being sucked back into my routine or typical behavior.

I'm going to wrap up by saying this, "Give freely and forgive quickly." It came to me as I was waking up from a dream and I had to write it down. It's important to forgive yourself for everything you've done and expand that forgiveness to everyone you know, past and present. People are just doing what they think is right at the time. They are also constantly learning from their mistakes and trying to do what they think is better. In short, we are all capable of change and I think that interacting with people who are trying to embrace these key things in their lives is the best medicine to which anyone could be exposed.

Chapter 16: Different Paths

December 19, 2006

It would seem that we are all on different paths in life. There are no two people alike, and no two paths just alike in life. We're all striving for something using our own set of beliefs to determine the best way to get there, and we like to seek out people who share similar paths. We enjoy being in their company and sharing stories about our common path. But no matter what paths we share with others, ours is still a little different. This makes it difficult to identify fully with another person and can often lead to misunderstandings or conflict.

However, we are all, in fact, on the same overall path to happiness. We're all divinely complex beings getting through life the best we know how, whether we realize it or not. Therein, lies the heart of learning unconditional compassion. I think that acknowledging the commonalities that link us all is the best way to make us better people.

The conflict and suffering that arise when we forget that we are all on a common path can be a vital teaching tool. If there were no suffering or conflict in the world around us, and in our personal lives, we wouldn't be challenged to strive for something. It would also make it more difficult to learn gratitude for all that we have to be thankful for, since we would lack a frame of reference.

An example of this has to do with the way the Buddha started his journey toward enlightenment. He was brought up in a luxurious environment insulated from the harsh world outside of the palace walls. When he was in his twenties, he was allowed to venture out into the world where he came face to face with suffering people for the first time. He was so overwhelmed with it that he left his family and kingdom behind in search of a reason why there was so much suffering in the world. I suspect, if he had never been confronted with suffering, he never would have found enlightenment, thereby changing the course of history dramatically.

So, suffering is never meaningless. It's a constant reminder that we are all human and prone to making mistakes. On a greater scale though, suffering can serve as a wake up call to the core love in us all that's just waiting to be let out. We have to love ourselves for doing the best we know how, and spread that love to everyone else doing the same thing, no matter how far off base they seem to be in our eyes.

Peace and love to you and yours during this holiday season, and may everything go exactly as it needs to for you to reach your ultimate potential. That's what's happening anyway, isn't it?

Chapter 17: Dealing with Negativity

January 7, 2007

Hopefully, everyone has gotten the new year off to a positive start and is gearing up for the best year you've experienced so far. I thought I might share some information that might make doing just that a little easier, if you're up for the challenge.

If you have people in your life that you dislike, it could be that what you dislike about someone else actually reflects something you dislike about yourself. I've come across this idea a couple of times and have actually seen it to be true in my life. However, it might be beneficial to fine tune this idea a bit.

If someone does something that elicits a "negative" emotion in you (anger, frustration, impatience, resentment, anxiety, etc.), that emotion is a signal for something you have not appropriately dealt with yet. I have found this to be true in my life, and have also noticed that it becomes a recurring event until it has been dealt with properly. Over time, it becomes obvious that there is something deeper at work that is trying to demand your attention.

So, if you are like me and are interested in being all that you can be, it's important for you to pay attention to these signals, which are expressed as thoughts and emotions. When something someone says or does triggers something you don't like in yourself (i.e. a negative emotion), pay attention. There is something which needs attention. Entire books have been written on the subject of how to deal with these emotions when they do arise, but one of the central proponents is to realize that your response is your choice. This is hard to come to grips with since we have developed well trained responses to certain stimuli, which often involves placing blame, but it is true.

So, when you encounter a situation that elicits one of these trained responses from you, such as anger, "choose" to respond differently. If, for example, your initial reaction is to defend yourself against a false accusation, stop and be with that feeling. Is it caused by injured pride or the need to never be in the wrong about something? Then, let it go rather than react. This gets back to an issue touched on in the book, *The Lost Art of Compassion*, involving graciously losing an argument. This may involve a bit of pride swallowing, and I can tell you from personal experience that pride is one of those things that does not taste all that good going down at first (it's an acquired taste).

However, if you are able to do this when your emotions flare, when the same trigger is encountered again it will have less of an affect on you. You are, in effect, changing your perspective on the issue and releasing the power it has over you. You are retraining yourself not to be negatively impacted by something someone else does or says.

It may help to ask yourself why something upsets you. It may also help to remind yourself that everyone is doing what they think is right at any given moment. It may help to try to see the issue from the other person's perspective. It may help to realize that everything will be just fine, regardless of the inconveniences encountered. It may help to remember that each little issue that prompts a response from us is a learning opportunity, and there will be plenty more if we don't get it right this time (be grateful when they occur).

The bottom line is that we are all divine beings in our own rights whether we realize it yet or not. If we can realize it in ourselves first, it's easier to see it in others.

Enjoy the new year to its fullest and do your best to make the most out of every day, even if it brings some minor inconveniences or hard lessons. We'll all be better off for it.

Chapter 18: Christianity

January 23, 2007

Religion is one of those subjects that I don't broach lightly, due to the fact that some people tend to have such deep rooted beliefs that saying something to the contrary has a tendency to upset them. But I have had three encounters now with Christian promotional materials which have given me some realizations about myself, as well as religion in general.

Let me start by saying, that I am one of those people who was turned off by Christianity a long time ago, due primarily to my exposure to televangelists who talked about eternal damnation for failing to follow certain rules. This idea of a vengeful and judgmental God has never really appealed to me, and unfortunately my view of Christianity has suffered as a result. I suspect that I am not alone in this and that those who have been condemning sinners to hell have actually been tarnishing the image of Christianity for a great number of people.

However, after two different eye catching pamphlets crossed my path in a week, both of which I read with an open mind, and both of which had the same elements of "believe or burn," I had a realization that made sense to me. I, finally, understood why "they" (the numerous authors, translators, editors, and promoters of the *Bible*) would make God out to be judgmental. "They" were/are trying to put the fear of God in people as an added incentive for people to follow the teachings of Jesus. This gave me a sense of relief because, I realized, "they" were only doing what they thought was best at the time (as I believe everyone is doing at all times).

However, I don't think that the best way to get people to become kind and caring people is by using fear tactics. I think that by projecting God to be judgmental, we ourselves become more judgmental. We are, in effect, justifying our own judgmental nature by making God in our image. This is where my third encounter with Christianity comes into play.

I received a DVD in the mail, and was given a second copy later by a friend, entitled "Jesus." It was apparently sent by a consortium of churches in the area. Not being particularly well versed in the life of Jesus, and being the open and eager to learn type of person I am, I watched the movie and took notes. I think the following quotes taken from the movie (which were supposed to be taken straight from the *Bible*) sum up the teachings of Jesus quite nicely:

> "Love your enemies. Be good to those who hate you. Bless those who curse you. Pray for those who mistreat you. If anyone strikes you on the one cheek, let him hit you on the other one also. If someone takes away your coat, let him have your shirt as well. Give to everyone who begs from you. And if someone takes what is yours, do not ask for it back again. Do for others as you would have others do for you.... Love your enemies and do good to them. And lend expecting nothing back. And then you will have a great reward.... Be merciful just as your father [God] is merciful. Judge not and you will not be judged. Condemn not and you will not be condemned. Forgive and you will be forgiven."
>
> *- The Jesus Film*, 1979

What a great message. It seems to me that if we could all live by these simple guidelines, which I hope represent the core essence of what it is to be a true Christian, then we would already be living in heaven. Another thing that fascinates me is that this message weaves throughout the Eastern religions as well. In fact, one of the main paths to enlightenment is paved by these same values. So, there must be something to it because I don't think that many ancient sages could be wrong ;-)

After watching the movie, I can even empathize with those people who would try to spread the word by any means necessary. But the means affect how the message is received, so great care should be taken when delivering it. In my personal opinion, now that Christianity's image has been tarnished in the minds of some, I think the only way to rectify the damage is to focus on embodying these core teachings.

In the end, I would not have even watched the movie a few short years ago, but I found it quite enlightening. I also felt like I had seen it once before a long time ago when I was too young to remember well. I was a bit turned off by the brief opening scene about Adam and Eve and "the Fall," but we'll get into that some other time.

Hope all is well with you and yours. Stay in touch, stay open minded, and love your enemies.

Chapter 19: Fear

February 3, 2007

Fear is a naturally occurring phenomenon that affects us all. It is a learned behavior that we encounter in our early years of development. It continues to surface throughout our lives until we deal with it and release it. It stems from the ego and its perceived separateness from everything around us. To quote an early lesson from *A Course in Miracles*, "A meaningless world engenders fear." But nothing in the world is meaningless. The only thing that's meaningless is all of the definitions we place on the world we see. Our own paradigms create our fear, when in fact there is nothing to fear.

This ties in with what Joseph Campbell says about Adam and Eve's fall from grace in the Garden of Eden. It is a symbolic representation of the loss of innocence of the fact that we are all one. Once we lose that innocence we are born with, fear steps in and the ego begins to take care of us, comforting us in our time of need and reinforcing our differences. As we become attached to our self-created identity, we become fearful of losing it and fearful of anything that conflicts with our personal belief system.

The upside to all of this is that fear can be overcome. Transcending our ego and returning to the innocence of Oneness is part of the key. Once we realize that there is no us and them, we can come to terms with all of our fears.

Some will say that some fears serve a natural purpose in ensuring our survival, and with this I can not argue. All I can venture forward is that fear may occur when confronted by a man eating lion, but that fear may lead to paralysis unless it is quickly transcended. Once that fear is overcome, clarity steps in to find more appropriate responses to potentially dangerous stimuli – fight or flight.

One of the things I have come to learn is that the fears we have today will continue to surface throughout our lives until we stop and look to the core of that fear and recognize it for what it is. According to David Hawkins and Eckhart Tolle, just to name a few, all fears come back to one central fear: the fear of death. This also gets back to our fear of losing our personal identity, which is synonymous with ego.

But that fear of death can be surrendered as an inevitability we all face, allowing us to live our lives to their fullest potential, not hampered by fear. The first step to fully surrender it, is to realize that all fear actually stems from a projection of what might happen in the future. Since we haven't died yet, we project our beliefs and ideas about it out there to help us cope with the fear of the unknown. But it will always remain unknown, which is actually what we fear the most.

Chapter 20: Breaking the Cycle

February 19, 2007

As you're probably aware, a lot of the things we do and say on a daily basis are done so out of habit. I have recently found a way that has helped me break out of the cycle of habitual doing, which increases my level of mindfulness and has some other hidden rewards.

When you feel compelled to do or say something, whether it's making a call, paying a bill, going to the refrigerator, walking the dog, or whatever; stop and ask yourself, "Do I really need to do/say that right now?" The answer to this question may be cloudy and may include rationalizations like, "Well if I don't do it now, I'm not going to do it." However, I always reassure myself that everything that needs to get done will, because that's the way it has always worked, and that I might actually benefit by pausing before acting.

Once you have asked yourself this question, do something different. This could be as simple as stopping to take a deep breath, sitting quietly for a moment, looking at your surroundings to appreciate their beauty, or whatever. The key here is to just break the routine by not immediately doing something out of habit (unless it's urgent).

Once you have taken a moment for yourself, before following the compulsive act in question, then go ahead and do whatever it is (unless you decide not to), but do it differently. For example, do it in slow motion. Do it in a different order than you normally would. Say something different than you would have said. Just do it in such a way that it takes the automation out of the action.

While trying to practice this, don't feel bad when you find yourself acting out of habit. When you catch it, just pause to reflect and find the humor in what you just did and the results it brought about. Realize you did it just out of habit and that it would have gotten done one way or the other. This is an effective practice in mindfulness and a good way to get to know yourself.

The real point is just to get you to start breaking free of acting out of habit. A lot of the things I feel compelled to do in a day just make my life more complicated than it needs to be. If I take a slightly more hands off approach, things still get done but with less stress on me and those around me. I'm not suggesting you do nothing, but do everything with more awareness.

I also wanted to mention that I recently finished the book, Way of the *Peaceful Warrior* by Dan Millman. I enjoyed the book quite a bit and included a quote from it below. I have also posted some of my favorite quotes on my blog. I hope you all are doing well and enjoying February to its fullest. It's over before you know it.

> "It is better for you to take responsibility for your life as it is, instead of blaming others, or circumstances, for your predicament. As your eyes open, you'll see that your state of health, happiness, and every circumstance of your life has been, in large part, arranged by you – consciously or unconsciously." (Page 28)
>
> - *Way of the Peaceful Warrior*, Dan Millman

Chapter 21: Allowing Peace

February 26, 2007

For those of you who are interested in obtaining an unprecedented level of internal peace, which would thereby create an environment of peace around you and ripple outward, I find the words of Eckhart Tolle quite simple and to the point. I'm finding myself fully in the present more and more often these days, but still being sucked into the old patterns of habitual reactions. Practice makes perfect as they say.

Tolle's website has numerous interviews that I am still reading through, but I have found his words to be quite powerful (especially when listened to on audio). To paraphrase what is quoted from an interview below, "If you just accept everything that happens to you without judgment, you no longer get upset when things don't go your way. When you just do your best and release your attachment to the outcome, it brings about an inner peace that dissolves all of your worries and anxieties about what the future may bring."

So next time you find yourself being cut off in traffic, spoken harshly to by someone, or in some other way hampered by events or other people, remember that everything happens of its own accord and that the majority of people are just going through life with blinders on, cruising on an autopilot programmed by their past experiences. They are not fully aware of the effect they have on the rest of the world as of yet and can not help doing what they do. It's not your job to fix them when it happens, just to accept them for who they are and don't take it personally. You will begin to feel more at peace and an increased level of happiness if you begin to practice what is suggested below. I know I have.

In the meantime, feel free to share this message with anyone you think might like the message it conveys, and/or email me with your feedback. I hope you have a great week and enjoy life and all it has to offer all of the time.

The Power of Now and the End of Suffering (Interview)

Sounds True (ST):

Being "in the present" sounds so obvious, and yet is quite hard to sustain. Do you have any practical tips for people for maintaining awareness of the present moment?

Eckhart Tolle (ET):

Although the old consciousness or rather unconsciousness still has considerable momentum and to a large extent still runs this world, the new awakened consciousness – presence – has already began to emerge in many human beings. In my book *The Power of Now*, I mention ways in which you can maintain present moment awareness, but the main thing is to allow this new state of consciousness to emerge rather than believe that you have to try hard to make it happen. How do you allow it to emerge? Simply by allowing this moment to be as it is. This means to relinquish inner resistance to what is – the suchness of now. This allows life to unfold beautifully. There is no greater spiritual practice than this.

ST: How much time and effort is required to realize "the power of now?" Can this really occur in an instant or is this the work of a lifetime?

ET: The power of now can only be realized now. It requires no time and effort. Effort means you're trying hard to get somewhere, and so you are not present, welcoming this moment as it is.

Whereas it requires no time to awaken – you can only awaken now – it does take time before you can stay awake in all situations. Often, you may find yourself being pulled back into old conditioned reactive patterns, particularly when faced with the challenges of daily living and of relationships. You lose the witnessing presence and become identified again with the "voice in the head," the continuous stream of thoughts, with its labels, judgments and opinions. You no longer know that they are only labels, judgments, and mental positions (opinions) – but completely believe in them. And so you create conflict. And then you suffer. And that suffering wakes you up again. Until presence becomes your predominant state, you may find yourself moving back and forth for a while between the old consciousness and the new, between mind identification and presence. "How long is it going to take?" is not a good question to ask. It makes you lose the now.

http://eckharttolle.com/home.php?section=news&type=News&show=NEWS%20-%20Interviews

Chapter 22: Acceptance of What Is

March 14, 2007

Let me start by saying that *Practicing the Power of Now* by Eckhart Tolle is a book that I strongly urge everyone in the world to read or listen to the audio version (I've listened to it twice now). I've been doing some very thorough reading for the last two years, and this work presents everything you need to know in a concise and easy to understand way, with specific techniques to practice in your daily life. It will change your life (and the lives of the people around you) for the better.

Having said all that, let me do my best to give you some helpful tid bits I've learned from it and some of Tolle's other works. Please don't take my words as a substitute for getting a copy of this book (in print or audio) as Tolle does a much better job of explaining it all.

Acceptance is the key to eliminating all of the pain, suffering, frustration, annoyance, etc. in your life. You may have a relatively happy life, but if you are like most people, and experience periods of time when you are dissatisfied in some way, shape, or form, it is a sign that you have not fully accepted "what is" in your life. Pain and suffering are caused by nonacceptance. If you are ready to be free of negativity, it's time to start practicing acceptance. I've been actively doing it for the last week or two and experiencing some very positive transformations. I've also realized that acceptance is a prerequisite to experiencing compassion because you can't feel compassion toward someone that you have not fully accepted for who they are.

Before I continue, do not mistake acceptance for becoming complacent. Just because you accept something does not mean you can not take action to make changes. You are not accepting a situation, you are accepting the "isness" of the current moment. Since you are powerless to change what has already happened, you can either react to it out of resistance (if you have not accepted it for what it is) or you can react to it from a place of acceptance, which leads you to a much more insightful and positive action (as opposed to a programmed reaction). Say "yes" to what is, then take action. Surrender to the way things are "in this moment" without judgment and inner peace naturally manifests.

As an example of this, we have several dogs and a new foster puppy who needs to be house trained. So, when the puppy poops in the house, I don't accept that there is poop in the house and leave it there. I accept that it has happened and take the necessary steps to fix the situation without judging myself or my wife for allowing it to happen, or the dog for making it happen. Taking steps to fix the problem from a place of acceptance makes cleaning up poop a much more tolerable task.

When you experience conditions in your life that seem to limit you in some way, realize that these are concealed openings into the formless state of peace for which you have been searching all these years (whether you realize it yet or not). Be grateful when you experience another frustration because you have been given yet another opportunity to practice acceptance. I know it may sound crazy to some who have a very challenging time, so it's important to start this practice with the little things in life that frustrate you.

You will begin to notice that there are recurring themes in your life that cause you frustration, and will continue to do so until you accept them and deal with them from a state of acceptance. When an opportunity arises to practice acceptance, notice how you feel (angry, sad, lonely, worried, etc.) and recognize it without judging yourself for feeling that way. This puts you in touch with who you truly are: the consciousness behind your thoughts, the silent observer. This opens the door for you to be more mindful of how your mind works and increases your awareness.

One final thing to remember in all of this involves staying present, or in the now. Stay out of the past and the future as often as possible when time is not necessary for practical purposes. Clock time involves setting a goal and focusing on each step as you work toward that goal and letting go of the outcome. Psychological time is the compulsive projection on the future goal and all of the possible outcomes (something I catch myself doing fairly often). We tend to use our past to create our identity and look toward the future for fulfillment, but remaining in the present brings us a sense of freedom. It takes practice to stay present, but I have seen first hand the positive impacts it can have.

As Tolle says, "Don't take my word for it. Try it for yourself." You will likely see that surrendering to what is, will transform you, which will in turn transform the world around you. You will naturally begin to attract less negativity as you free yourself from the power it has over you. Realize that most people around you have no choice in what they do because they are in an unconscious state (as we all are most of the time) and your resentment will disappear.

Chapter 23: Simple Tools for Seeing Goodness

March 20, 2007

We had a good discussion in the book group meeting I attended this past Monday night. We each discussed some of our favorite quotes from David Hawkins' 10 Simple Tools list (see list below). The idea was basically to pick one of these tools that resonates with you and apply it in your everyday life for a period of time and enjoy the results. In my last email I mentioned applying acceptance and the importance of that. Number 5 in the list below is basically the same concept because it involves forgiving everything that is witnessed.

I got to use a couple of them today while spending a brief while outside enjoying a beautiful Spring day. I was listening to birds sing as well as the heavy earth moving equipment going back and forth on the mountain behind our house. The rumble of the engine was easy enough to overlook but it was combined with periodic beeping noises when the equipment began backing up.

In order to come to terms with the constant beeping noise, which had the potential to disturb the peace if I allowed it to, I decided to find the beauty in the noise (number 4 below). Surprisingly, it was not hard at all. All I had to do was imagine how many lives were lost in construction related accidents from people being backed over by drivers who could not see them. Once I began to appreciate how many lives have been spared as a result of this simple invention (a beeping reverse), I began to really appreciate and accept the noise as a wonderful thing.

Once I came in and looked at the daily quote from the Dalai Lama, I saw how appropriate it all was. "To deepen your gratitude toward all people, it is helpful to reflect on the unintended kindness of those who provide goods and services without necessarily knowing the names or faces of those whom they serve. In this life there are so many facilities we enjoy–nice buildings, roads, and so forth–that are produced by other people." I have become more proficient at seeing the good in people and can more easily think of the positive things that can result from disastrous events, which makes everything easier to accept.

The tools below are great and you might end up using one or more of them in any given situation. They really drive home the importance of the unconditionalness required to find true peace within yourself. I hope you enjoy.

(By the way. If you catch yourself judging someone or something harshly, try to look for something to be grateful for so that you can fully accept it. Then, be grateful for the opportunity to live up to your life's challenge.)

1.   Be kind to everything and everyone, including oneself, all the time, with no exception.

2.   Revere all of life in all its expressions, no matter what, even if one does not understand it.

3.   Presume no actual reliable knowledge of anything at all. Ask God [higher self, all that is, etc.] to reveal its meaning.

4.   Intend to see the hidden beauty of all that exists–it then reveals itself.

5.   Forgive everything that is witnessed and experienced, no matter what. Remember Christ, Buddha, and Krishna all said that all error is due to ignorance. Socrates said all men can choose only what they believe to be the good.

6.   Approach all of life with humility and be willing to surrender all positionalities and mental/emotional arguments or gain.

7.   Be willing to forgo all perceptions of gain, desire, or profit and thereby be willing to be of selfless service to life in all of its expressions.

8.   Make one's life a living prayer by intention, alignment, humility, and surrender. True spiritual reality is actually a way of being n the world.

9. By verification, confirm the levels of consciousness and spiritual truth of all teachers, teachings, spiritual groups, and literature with which one intends to be aligned or a student.

10. Accept that by spiritual declaration, commitment, and surrender, Knowingness arises that provides support, information, and all that is needed for the entire journey.

Transcending the Levels of Consciousness,
David Hawkins (Page 335)

Chapter 24: The World Revolves Around Me (and You)

April 3, 2007

Thanks to my growing level of mindfulness, I've caught myself doing something I think I have been doing all of my life – looking for reasons for everything. After finding myself doing it a few times, I discovered why it is I seem to always be looking for reasons. The bottom line of the search seems to be to find something to blame, or attribute things to. Or, possibly to escape blaming myself for a particular event. At first I thought I was just searching for patterns, but then I realized that the patterns being sought did in fact have a common thread – I wanted to discover why something is the way it is so that I can rest assured that it's not my fault.

Well, I have stopped doing that. I have now come to the realization that the entire world already revolves around me, and that I am the cause behind every event in my life. These different forms that come into my awareness all day long are all being put there by me, and they are being put there because they are exactly what I need to encounter in order to increase my level of awareness. For the past thirty plus years I haven't been giving each event its due, but I have decided to change all of that now.

Since I no longer have anyone else to blame for anything that happens to me, I am now free to use each life event to get me further down the path I am traveling, rather than getting bogged down in the search for ways to ensure I'm right and that someone or something else is wrong. A great weight has been lifted and I now see the world through different colored glasses. Ones that are not tinted by the film of self- rightfulness. I am now grateful for every event that happens to me, knowing that there are no "bad" things.

When confronted by a difficult situation, I will be looking for the lessons I have not yet learned from countless previous encounters with that situation. I will be grateful for the opportunity to respond appropriately this time, and therefore grateful for everything that happens to me at every turn. I will also do my best to help others along if they are in need of help because that is ultimately what I feel drawn to do.

I will take every ache, pain, misstep, awkward moment, pause, negative emotion, naughty thought, as well as, every peaceful moment or beautiful scene as a reminder to be present in this moment and practice acceptance for all that is. I will not judge myself harshly when I fail to live up to the high standard I have set, and will treat myself compassionately if I find my mind wandering counterproductively. I will also treat others with that same level of compassion with which I treat myself, knowing that they too are human.

I will sit with and observe each negative emotion that occurs in my life from the standpoint of the observer behind my thoughts, because I know this to be the way to make negativity dissolve. For there are no negative situations, only negative thoughts about situations.

All of the pain and anger in the world is simply caused by a mental position being perpetually fed by all of the information we amass regarding who is to blame for what, so that we can maintain our own secure place of always being right. I am no longer afraid to be wrong and will admit it when I am (sometimes even when I know I'm not), because I know that in the grand scheme of things, it really doesn't matter. "So what," and "Big deal," will be the things I say to the things that used to get me worked up, because I am the one who gave them power over me.

In short, I'm free at last, thank God Almighty I'm free at last!

After I wrote that, I cried and laughed at the same time and felt too moved to go back and fix any typos. I hope you in-joy :-)

Chapter 25: It's All Necessary

May 2, 2007

I wanted to share something with you that I have trouble remembering in my daily life, but when I do remember it life becomes much more pleasant all the way around. If you can remember this always, I think you will see the same results I do.

Everything that is happening right now, to you personally as well as anywhere in the world, is absolutely necessary for our evolution, and evolution is absolutely necessary for our very survival. Therefore, everything happening right now is critical to our survival, as was everything that ever happened in the past. It's all necessary and accepting the necessity of it is the key to transcending pain and suffering.

This does not mean you have to sit back and do nothing about what's going on. Quite the contrary. When something happens that you see as being "wrong," the first step is to accept that it is happening or has happened rather than just reacting to it. Once you have accepted what is happening, you can decide to act to rectify the situation and your actions will be magnified in their intensity and effectiveness. This is because you will not be acting from a place of frustration, resistance, and negativity, which taints your actions with negativity. Instead you will be reacting from a place of non-judging acceptance and understanding, which by itself radiates a kind of peacefulness and power. As I've said many times before, acceptance is the key to it all.

Chapter 26: It's About Time

May 31, 2007

I hope you are enjoying everything you are engaged in on a daily basis and bringing more awareness to the thoughts rolling around in your head. If you are, I'm sure you have noticed some very interesting things about how your mind works. One of the things I'm noticing is how much time I spend thinking about something that has already happened or thinking about something that hasn't happened yet (and may not even happen). It's interesting to witness what happens when you become the witness of these thoughts rather than being completely immersed in them. I'll share more about this at a later present moment, but in the mean "time", I wanted to share a few things about time that might interest you.

I've been reading this interesting book called *Exploring the Sky* (Richard Moreshl) which has quite a few projects involving the objects in space we see from Earth, as well as historic information about how ancient people used the sky to guide them. So far there is a lot of information about how the passage of time was determined based on the changes observed in the stars, moon, sun, and various other objects. One project in the book involved building a nocturnal time piece which consists of a circle with tick marks for months and hours along with a couple of pointers. To use it you center the hole in the center with the North Star and line up the markers with two stars in the Big Dipper and you can tell what month and hour it is (in the Northern Hemisphere).

There is a great deal written about the evolution of other time keeping devices as well. One thing that I found interesting is that minutes were not measured on clocks until a little over 300 years ago. Imagine a life without minutes :-) Prior to that only hours were tracked and before that only days, etc. It's obvious from what I have read so far that human fascination with time has been around for thousands of years. But I thought it was all summed up nicely by a quote from H. W. Longfellow:

Notes to Self

WHAT IS TIME?

The shadow on the dial
The striking of the clock
The running of the sand
Day and Night, Summer and Winter
Months, Years, Centuries–
These are but arbitrary and
outward signs, the measure
of time, not time itself.
Time is the life of the Soul.

To me this means that clock time is but a figment of our imagination that helps us measure changes, but that real time is the eternal and changeless part of our essence. Time is just a label we put on the ever changing present moment in which we find ourselves. (As an interesting aside, when I was a teenager I had a foretaste of this realization when I decided time was just a well crafted conspiracy to sell clocks).

As Eckhart Tolle likes to point out, nothing ever happened in the past. It happened in the now. Nothing will ever happen in the future. It will happen in the now. Everything always happens in the present moment. Even if you experience something 20 years from now, you will be experiencing it in the present moment. As you can see, this makes the present moment ever lasting and all you will ever have. So why not enjoy it?

If you are still unsure about how you can enjoy the present moment and still get things done that you need to get done, I suggest the book I have been suggesting for a while now, *Practicing the Power of Now* (or even *The Power of Now*), as it clearly addresses these issues. However, I will also continue to share my own observations on how you can bring your awareness back to the present moment to make the most of the only thing you will ever have.

Chapter 27: Preconceived Notions

June 7, 2007

If you're like me, you have a large stock pile of preconceived notions about things. These are the ideas and standards we have for judging people, events, places, etc. For example, we have preconceived notions about what makes a person a good person, which is broken down into countless categories depending on a person's role (i.e. what makes a parent a good parent, what makes a friend a good friend, what makes a teacher a good teacher, what makes a leader a good leader, etc.). Of course these preconceived notions are not limited to people. We have them about everything from what foods taste good to what careers are worthwhile to pursue.

These notions, conceived in the past, are influenced by our upbringing, social and cultural environment, as well as our own egoic drive to have an opinion or view point about everything. We feel that these preconceived notions are our survival tools that keep us safe and happy, and we can rationalize hundreds of ways in which our lives have been made better by having them. The truth is that we are clinging to them out of fear, the fear of being lost without them. They make up our ego, our perceived identity, which is a mind made self that separates and differentiates us from the world around us. But this perceived separation is actually what leads to various levels of suffering or discontent in our lives.

These preconceived notions control how we see the world around us. Since they are the yardstick by which we judge other people and situations, they keep us stuck in the past and cloud our judgement of the present. The past then perpetuates itself through this dense filter made up of past experiences (our mind) into the future. This is why we continue to manifest repetitive patterns in our lives or still feel the same after something in our life situation changes (i.e. a new job, a new home, etc.). In effect, our judgments and preconceived notions are creating our future to be just as it was in the past.

Judging others based on our preconceived notions is one of the major obstacles preventing us from obtaining happiness, but it is what we have relied on our whole lives to bring about just that. So how do we overcome this habitual practice of judging everyone and everything that comes into our lives and break free of the past? Well, it doesn't happen overnight, at least not for most, but there are some basic practices you can start right now that make it happen.

First, start becoming aware of your own judgements when they occur. Be on the look out for feelings of negativity as they are good indications that your judgements have taken over. Recognize that these feelings of frustration are based on preconceived notions that you still hold to be true. Don't judge yourself for judging, just acknowledge that your past conditioning has shown up for you to notice.

Then, recognize that not everyone sees the world the same way you do. That is, no one else has the same preconceived notions as you. In fact, there is no limit to the differentiation among people and their collective opinions. We are all as unique as our fingerprints, and no two life situations (past or present) are the same. That diversity is what makes life interesting, and is something for which to be grateful rather than frustrated.

It's also important to look deeper than the outer layer of personality to see that we are all exactly alike. We have all created our own way in the world with the hope that we will find true happiness. That's all anyone wants. We do what we do, say what we say, act the way we act because we believe that is the best way to bring about happiness. This cycle applies to everyone of us, therefore the judgement you place on someone else could just as accurately be placed on yourself.

Practice being the watcher, or listener, of the thoughts in your head. Pay attention as often as you can to the thoughts in your head. At first you can use key events as reminders to pay attention to your thoughts. For example, when you find yourself judging a person or event, or you find yourself formulating an opinion on a subject, or when you find yourself defending an opinion or getting upset, just pay attention to the thoughts. Don't judge yourself for having the thoughts, just listen impartially. If you find yourself having internal conversations about random things (as I find myself doing a lot), just bring your awareness to the thoughts and recognize them as just thoughts. There's nothing personal about them, so don't beat yourself up for having them.

You can also do this when engaged in conversations with other people. Instead of constantly focusing on how you are going to respond, just listen to them with your full attention. All of this can be called practicing presence or mindfulness and is the first step in awakening, which releases you from the control the past has over you. I think you will like the results, but I'd love to hear how it goes.

Chapter 28: Political Reconciliation

June 22, 2007

I've been trying to stay relatively uninvolved in political goings on for a long time now, but I'm still on email lists of various activist groups that I joined during my outrage over stolen elections, the war, etc.. This does not mean I have become complacent, however. I've learned enough to know that I am doing the one thing I can truly do to make the world a better place by increasing my level of awareness and presence. True activism must come from a place of oneness and non-ego in order for it not to continue to feed the negativity which is being fought.

For example, if you "love" the green power initiative, but "hate" those contributing to contamination of the environment, then everything you do to fight for that initiative is tainted with the negative energy that is creating that which you are fighting. The same is true for any issue whether it be the war or something else. I ran across this quote in *The Power of Now* that sums it up nicely, "If you fight madness, you become mad yourself."

Consequently, I have remained relatively quiet despite constant email calls to take action regarding this or that. I have also remained fairly informed about what is going on in the world, however, and I have been recognizing the true nature of the issues causing the pain and suffering in the world at this time. This is where reconciliation comes in.

I have mixed feelings about sharing this type of information because of the negativity it may bring, but I know that many people may feel that what I have been sharing over the last year or so does not "fit" with what's going on in the world. Hopefully broaching this subject will illustrate how these teachings apply to the current world situation, and shed some light on what each one of us can do to bring about positive change (which is all anyone truly wants). With that in mind, read on and know that I will close on a very optimistic note.

Based on an investigative report from the BBC, there is a very strong connection between the Iraq war and big oil companies (I can hear the exaggerated gasps of shock from some of you now). The gist of the story is that the Bush administration had planned on privatizing the oil in Iraq once Saddam was taken out of power. However, Exxon Mobile's lead attorney threatened to sue if they did that, then proposed that the Iraq oil supply be "controlled." The end result would mean higher gas prices and higher profits for big oil companies. Everyone else, whether that be the gas buying public or the people of Iraq, suffer as a result of a decision based on selfish greed.

At about the same time I read this report on the oil connection, I received an email from the mother of an Iraq war veteran whose son came back in a bad state. He was suffering from severe PTSD and was having difficulty receiving the care he needed from the VA. She mentioned in her email that many of the friends her son served with in Iraq were coming home and either committing suicide, becoming abusive to their wives and children, or getting hooked on alcohol and other drugs. As a result, this woman had been living in a state of fear that her son may commit suicide. She was camping out in Washington DC in an attempt to bring an end to the war and make sure veterans received proper care once they returned from war.

After reading her email, I felt compelled to help, so I offered to send her son a copy of *Practicing the Power of Now* to help him break free of the past (the author, Eckhart Tolle, was also on the verge of suicide when his life changing event occurred). She gave me his mailing address and I mailed him a copy. I have not heard from him but I can only hope that it will help in some small way.

There are countless other examples of corruption and the toll it takes on human lives, now and throughout history. So, how do I reconcile all of this madness? I recognize it all for what it truly is – unconsciousness. The people in positions of power who appear to be profiting from this war at the expense of other peoples' lives are after the same thing the rest of us are after – happiness. They naively think that more power and money will bring them what they seek.

However, no matter how many billions of dollars they accumulate, it's still not enough. The fact that they won't find happiness in material wealth will probably only create more internal suffering for them. I also suspect there are many profiteers who are not totally blind to the misery being caused by their quest, which may lead to even more internal conflict unless they are able to rationalize away the need to feel compassion for others. I think it's safe to say that some of the world's most unhappy people are also some of the wealthiest. Their hearts still feel empty despite all of the worldly goods.

Many people still believe that money is the key to happiness, and that if you just made a bit more, everything would be alright (I still feel like that from time to time). But, it doesn't really matter how much money you have if you are still in an unconscious, or ego dominated, state of mind. The more you make, the more you spend, and you stay in the exact same place with more "stuff" to show for it. That is until you change what's on the inside, which is where everything on the outside is created.

My invitation to you is to not fall into the trap of resenting government officials and oil executives for their lack of consideration for the suffering being inflicted, so that they can find the fulfillment that they will never find, and to remember that this resentment only breeds more negativity. If we take a more compassionate attitude toward these people, without judgement or blame, we bring much needed positive energy into the world necessary to create true change.

We, as a collective population, have been recreating the same mistakes over and over again for a long time now. This is true on a global level as well as an individual level. So why does history seem to be repeating itself? We haven't learned our lesson yet and life keeps giving us new opportunities to do just that. In fact, life's true purpose is to awaken us from our unconscious madness before we destroy ourselves.

However, in order for a great number of people to awaken, the world situation will likely have to deteriorate more and more. Some people are easier than others to "wake up," but each time a new person wakes up, it creates a ripple effect that raises the energy level everywhere, increasing the likelihood that more will awaken.

Do you want to save the planet? Start by having compassion for those who are still destroying it, and do not view yourself to be superior to anyone else. We are all one inseparable energetic organism and you are just looking at different forms of yourself in others. We all need to be seen for whom we truly are in order to awaken and stop the madness.

Chapter 29: Blame - Don't Take it Personally

June 29, 2007

One day, on my way into a local supermarket I frequent, I paused at a table out front taking signatures on a petition for something. While I was there an employee was returning from her lunch break and paused to relay a story to the person next to me. She was saying that her day had taken a turn for the worse when one of the customers threw money at her rather than just handing it to her. She was upset by that because she felt she had done nothing to deserve such a thing.

After I had done my shopping I ended up in her line. I jokingly forewarned her that once she told me my total I was going to throw my money at her. She smiled and thanked me for the forewarning. When it came time to pay I just handed it to her and said I couldn't bring myself to do it. She laughed and said that she later realized that the customer's behavior probably didn't have anything to do with her and that she shouldn't have taken it personally. I agreed and wished her a better day to come.

It later dawned on me that her insight into the situation was quite profound. We are so prone to take everything personally that it distorts our thinking. We, then, tend to blame others for any negative feelings or emotions we experience by being exposed to their behavior. This brings me to a lovely little email from Daily Om I received the other day that sums up dealing with such feelings nicely. It is entitled, *Burdensome Feelings*.

"As we begin to truly understand that the world outside of us is a reflection of the world inside of us, we may feel confused about who is to blame for the problems in our lives. If we had a difficult childhood, we may wonder how we can take responsibility for that, and in our current relationships, the same question arises. We all know that blaming others is the opposite of taking responsibility, but we may not understand how to take responsibility for things that we don't truly feel responsible for. We may blame our parents for our low self-esteem, and we may blame our current partner for exacerbating it with their unconscious behavior. Objectively, this seems to make sense. After all, it is not our fault if our parents were irresponsible or unkind, and we are not to blame for our partner's bad behavior.

Perhaps the problem lies with the activity of blaming. Whether we blame others or blame ourselves, there is something aggressive and unkind about it. It sets up a situation in which it becomes difficult to move forward under the burdensome feelings of shame and guilt that arise. It also puts the resolution of our pain in the hands of someone other than us. Ultimately, we cannot insist that someone else take responsibility for their actions; only they can make that choice when they are ready. In the meantime, if we want to move forward with our lives instead of waiting around for something that may or may not happen, we begin to see the wisdom of taking the situation into our own hands.

We do this by forgiving our parents, even if they have not asked for our forgiveness, so that we can be free. We end the abusive relationship with our partner, who may never admit to any wrongdoing, because we are willing to take responsibility for how we are treated. In short, we love ourselves as we want to be loved and create the life we know we deserve. We leave the resolution of the wrongs committed against us in the hands of the universe, releasing ourselves to live a life free of blame."

http://www.dailyom.com/cgi-
bin/display/printerfriendly.cgi?articleid=9097

There is another part to this that I hope to add to later. In the meantime I would like to wish you the best. And remember, don't take anything personally, or better yet, practice not taking your thoughts too seriously. These are wonderfully liberating practices.

Chapter 30: Beliefs Lead to Suffering

July 14, 2007

I just finished a wonderful book called *A Thousand Names for Joy*. It's by a lady named Byron Katie who "woke up to reality" (a.k.a. became enlightened, self-realized, etc.) back in the mid eighties. I was previously unaware of her work, but am grateful that a friend suggested this book. It's so nice to get a female perspective, and an altogether different perspective, on what it's like to be enlightened and how we can all "get there." It's also wonderful to see how much it agrees with Eckhart Tolle. The bottom line is that acceptance of what is will set you free.

Katie, as she likes to be called, had the following observation about life after she awakened, which, by the way, took place while she was living in a halfway house for women, depressed to the point of being suicidal (a state that many enlightened folks underwent before their transition).

> "I discovered that when I believed my thoughts, I suffered, but that when I didn't believe them, I didn't suffer, and that this is true for every human being. Freedom is as simple as that. I found that suffering is optional. I found a joy within me that has never disappeared, not for a single moment. That joy is in everyone, always."
>
> *A Thousand Names for Joy*, Byron Katie (Preface)

She quickly developed what she calls The Work, which is a series of four questions that she uses to put thoughts and beliefs to the test, thereby transcending their hold on us. The Work has gained widespread popularity and she has been traveling the world to bring it to people everywhere (see www.thework.com for more information). The four questions are:

1. Is it true?
2. Can I absolutely know that it is true?

3. How do I react when I believe this thought?
4. Who would I be without the thought?

The steps are then followed by a turn around where various opposites of the thought are stated to see that there may be truth in the opposite of the truth, or at least see how we feel when we choose to believe the opposite of what we believe. The goal is finding the truth behind what we believe to be the truth.

As luck would have it, I soon encountered a life situation that allowed me to see the truth of the Work in action. It happened while my wife and I were dining outside at one of our favorite local restaurants. Some people sitting nearby on the patio had a couple of well behaved dogs with them (the restaurant typically allows dogs on the patio so it was not an uncommon sight). At one point, one of the dogs decided to take issue with the waiter and began barking at him. The waiter quelled him with a treat and we all continued about our business. The dog barked a few more times at the same waiter, who continued to try to make friends with the dog. Eventually they figured out that it was the waiter's hat that was making the dog uneasy and things settled down.

However, during this period of time one of the diners complained about the presence of the dog to their waiter. Management was notified and the waiters were debating whether to ask the couple to remove the dog or just let them finish and leave (they were almost finished with their meal). The dog had settled down and none of the other diners were really bothered by his occasional outbursts while he was having them.

When the couple finally left, the man who had complained began clapping very loudly, I suspect hoping that he would be the start of a wave of applause throughout the patio. He was the only one who was so inclined and I suspect I was not alone in finding his behavior more disturbing than that of the barking dog.

As if that were not enough excitement for one evening, a little while later the couple at the table next to us began to wonder where their food was. They asked their waiter about the status and indicated that they were there before someone else who had just gotten served. He went back to check the status and came back empty handed. Before he could get the words, "Here's what happened..." out of his mouth the man at the table stood up abruptly and said, "We have to leave! Come on, let's go!" the waiter was trying to apologize for the mix up that had occurred in the kitchen, but the man didn't want to hear it. His female companion was calmly explaining that they were very disappointed while the man was saying, "And your food isn't really that good either!"

As you can see, it was quite an evening. It made me tense witnessing both of these encounters and left me with an internal cringe that lasted a while. However, as I found myself confronted with passing judgement on these people, I immediately realized that their suffering was based on their beliefs about the way life should be. One man believed that the dog was a nuisance and that dogs should not be allowed on the patio. So it was not the dog's presence that upset him, it was his thoughts about the dog's presence. The couple next to us believed that they should have been served before someone who came in after them, which brought about their anger.

It helped me see that these real world examples of suffering are caused by all of the beliefs we have accumulated throughout our lives, but what's more important is what I got to witness in myself (where it all begins). My initial impressions of the man clapping, and the man leaving in a huff would have been, "What an asshole." However, I accepted that they were doing only what they felt was right at the time thinking it would bring about what they wanted – to feel better.

I decided to look at the feeling of uneasiness that I had experienced to see why it was there. I was obviously made uncomfortable by the conflict but what thoughts did I have that might bring this about? Here was a chance for me to do the Work on myself.

It occurred to me that the reaction I experienced had to do with the belief that people should be more tolerant. So, I put that to the test to see what would happen.

People should be more tolerant.

1. Is it true? Yes.

2. Can I absolutely know that it is true? Well, it seems true. The only thing that makes me hesitate from saying it's absolutely true is that people are all on their own path and can not help it if they are not yet aware of the fact that their intolerance is causing them pain. So I guess I can not know for sure that everyone should be more tolerant even if it seems like a good idea.

3. How do I react when I believe that people should be more tolerant and they're not? I become uncomfortable. I become worried. I get angry and indignant and judgmental.

4. Who would I be without the thought, "People should be more tolerant?" I would be more accepting of others. I would not have internal conflict. I would feel more at ease, even happier.

Now turn it around. "People should not be more tolerant." Instead, "They should be just the way they are now." People already are as tolerant as they should be. "I should be more tolerant." The truth comes out in this step and the problem is realized to be one inside me and not caused by others. My lack of tolerance for less than tolerant people creates more intolerance in the world and makes me feel stressed when I am exposed to intolerance, thereby pushing me further away from accepting what is. It's simple but powerful Work that helps set us free from the thoughts that keep us from realizing our full potential. See what you think.

Here are some inspiring quotes from *A Thousand Names for Joy*, by Byron Katie:

> The apparent craziness of the world, like everything else, is a gift that we can use to set our minds free. Any stressful thought that you have about the planet, for example, shows you where you are stuck, where your energy is being exhausted in not fully meeting life as it is, without conditions. You can't free yourself by finding a so-called

enlightened state outside your own mind. When you question what you believe, you eventually come to see that you are the enlightenment you've been seeking. Until you can love what is–everything, including the apparent violence and craziness–you're separate from the world, and you'll see it as dangerous and frightening. I invite everyone to put these fearful thoughts on paper, question them, and set themselves free. When mind is not at war with itself, there's no separation in it. I'm sixty-three years old and unlimited. If I had a name, it would be Service. If I had a name, it would be Gratitude. (Page 87)

All fear is like this. It's caused by believing what you think–no more, no less. It's always the story of a future. If you want fear on purpose, get a plan. Fear is not possible when you've questioned your mind; it can be experienced only when the mind projects the story of a past into a future. The story of a past is what enables us to project a future. If we weren't attached to the story of a past, our future would be so bright, so free, that we wouldn't bother to project time. We would notice that we're already living in the future, and that it's always now. (Page 136)

The Great Way is easy. It's what reveals itself right here, right now. "Do the dishes." "Answer the email." "Don't answer the email." It's the great Way because it's the only way. Whatever you do or don't do is your contribution to reality. Nothing could be easier. Nothing else is required; you can't do it wrong. (Page 155)

She lets all things come because here they come anyway; it's not as if she had a choice. She lets all things go because there they go, with or without her consent. She delights in the coming and the going. Nothing comes until she needs it, nothing goes until it's no longer needed. She is very clear about this. Nothing is wasted; there's never too much or too little. (Page 177)

When you hide your flaws, you teach us to hide ours. I love to say that we are just waiting for one teacher, just one, to give us permission to be who we are now. You appear as this, big or small, straight or bent. That's such a gift to give. The pain is in withholding it. Who else is going to give us permission to be free, if not you? Do it for your own sake, and we'll follow. We're a reflection of your thinking, and when you free yourself, we all become free. (Page 193)

When you revere a spiritual teacher, it's yourself that you're revering, because you can't project anything but yourself... It's a fine thing to love Jesus [or Buddha], but until you can love the monster, the terrorist, the child molester, until you can meet your worst enemy without defense or justification, your reverence for Jesus [or Buddha] isn't real, because each of these is just another of his forms. That's how you know when you are truly revering your spiritual teacher; when your reverence goes across the board. (Page 240)

I trust everyone. I trust them to do what they do, and I'm never disappointed. And since I trust people, I know to let them find their own way. The wonderful thing about inquiry is that there's no one to guide you but you. There's no guru, no teacher who, in her great wisdom, shows you the answers. Only your own answers can help you. You yourself are the way and the truth and the life, and when you realize this, the world becomes very kind. (Page 247)

We think that because Jesus and the Buddha wore robes and owned nothing, that's how freedom is supposed to look. But can you live a normal life and be free? Can you do it from here, right now? That's what I want for you. We have the same desire: your freedom. And I love that you're attached to material objects, whether you have them or not, so that you can come to realize that all suffering comes from the mind, not the world. (Page 252)

The litmus test for self-realization is a constant state of gratitude. This gratitude is not something you can look for or find. It comes from another direction, and it takes you over completely. It's so vast that it can't be dimmed or overlaid. (Page 27)

Chapter 31: What Am I?

August 30, 2007

Have you ever asked yourself, "What am I, truly?" and then sought to actually find the answer? This is something suggested by Adyashanti, who is another enlightened teacher who takes a straight up, no holds barred approach to teaching people to find themselves. With this particular approach (which is also referred to as the direct method), you sit quietly and clear your head of thoughts (or ignore the ones that inevitably come up) and ask yourself some serious questions, then feel or experience the answer as opposed to thinking about it. Here are some of the questions I have been using in my practice: "What am I? What is it that is seeing these things around me? What is it that's underneath or behind all of my thoughts and ideas about the world? What is truly behind my eyes looking out on the world?" I invite you to focus all of your attention on finding what it is that is really here underneath it all.

The idea is to connect with what is below or behind your senses, to what it is that is truly experiencing them. Do not use the mind to label the things you are looking at, and let go of the thoughts you have about them as you focus your attention on that which is experiencing the world around you. As you do this, you will likely see that it is not a "who" that is experiencing these things, but a "what."

The mind may cover up the answer as it tries to remain the primary interpreter of the forms around you, but if you spend a couple of minutes focusing ever more deeply into what is really here, you will likely find that there is nothing here but a presence, a stillness, consciousness itself. This is what you truly are – pure awareness. When you do this, you are turning your awareness back on itself, and, in so doing, becoming aware of your inner self. This is where our ultimate search for truth eventually leads – inside.

Another thing you might also discover while connecting with your inner self (after doing it a time or two) is that this presence within you is also all around you. It permeates that which you are, as well as, that which you are seeing, hearing, feeling, etc. It's all around you, as well as, within you. It has no borders. It's always there and never goes away. Thoughts may hide it from view, but it's ever present and it's what connects us all. It's what we all have in common, and can be accessed at anytime.

Having spent some time lately just being, I can safely say that it is a very peaceful state. This is where all of the truly powerful teachings point and I now have a far better grasp of what it is all about, despite my mind's constant drive to try to understand, analyze or describe it. Rather than go on I will just suggest that you try looking into what you truly are for yourself and see what you find.

Chapter 32: Conditional Happiness - War and Peace

September 17, 2007

Many of us are in states of conditional happiness, or at least contentment, a good deal of the time (some more often than others). This means that as long as things are going our way, or our life situation meets a certain list of criteria we have set up as prerequisites for happiness, we are happy or at peace. This manifests as people making sure these criteria are met and doing what they think will set the stage for continued happiness. But when things are not going our way, or certain criteria are lacking, we tend to be unhappy. This unhappiness, in whatever form it takes, is a form of war. We are at war with the way things currently are.

If we take the state of the war in Iraq as an example of this phenomenon, we see a country in chaos and conflict. We also have many people divided over the best way to proceed to bring an end to this war. As human beings, we all want stability and peace but different people have different ideas about what peace looks like and how to bring about peace. Some think that using force to defeat those who oppose peace will bring about peace. Some think walking away from the conflict is the best way to bring about peace. There are obviously several different variations of these approaches, but in the end no one really knows for sure what will result in peace.

War in the world leads to personal wars with what is. Many who are opposed to the war are struggling to bring an end to it as best they know how. Their happiness is currently contingent (at least in part) upon bringing an end to a war that has taken countless lives and promises to take countless more before it is all over. Many of those people believe that bringing home troops will bring about the end of the war and an end to their personal struggle and eventually happiness in their lives.

For others, their happiness may be somewhat contingent on bringing peace to Iraq by defeating those who are disrupting the peace. They hope to beat back the insurgents so that the Iraqi people can regain control of the peace themselves. These people are engaged in a personal war to see the outer war won and brought to a peaceful close.

In many respects, these two different camps of people are at war with each other because they see the opposing side as a hindrance to the closure they are seeking. They see the opposition as an obstacle to the personal happiness they are seeking. Those who disrupt our personal peace are often seen as the cause for our suffering.

In reality, the world we see around us is actually a mirror reflecting back what is going on inside us at any moment in time. This outer war, currently being fought predominantly in Iraq, serves as an example of the inner war we experience when things are not going our way. We are at war with what is and want to bring about peace through manipulating our outer environment. However, we can not always control our outer circumstances, and if we could, there would inevitably be someone with a different idea of what is needed for happiness who would disrupt our status quo. Therefore, being in a state of conditional happiness, the kind that only happens when everything lines up just right, guarantees you will be unhappy.

Can we achieve a state of permanent, unconditional happiness? If so, what can we do to bring about the permanent peace we all desire? What are your feelings about the answers to these two questions? We all have an arsenal of beliefs we have cultivated over the years that we are likely to turn to for help when asked questions like this. But beliefs are ineffectual when searching for truth as they keep you stuck in the past, where they were originally formed.

First, you have to ask yourself if you really want to live in a permanent and unconditional state of peace and happiness. Some may have enough conditional happiness in their lives that they don't feel the need for more at this time, especially considering that they may have to give up some of those beliefs and judgments they have been protecting (and seemingly been protected by) for so many years.

If you do want permanent peace in your life, look at those things that seem to disrupt your peace rather than avoid them. Your greatest teachers are often those who cause you stress, make you angry or create tension. These things are pointing you toward unresolved issues in your own life. Look deeply at the true cause for negative feelings to see if there is something there of any substance. More often than not, all you will find are thoughts and beliefs about the way things are "supposed" to be.

When you find these thoughts, try doing The Work on them. Ask yourself: Is this (thought, belief, idea, statement) true? Can I really know if it is true? How do I feel when I believe this thought? What would I be without this thought? Then turn around the thought or belief to see if the opposite is more true than the thought with which you started. Byron Katie suggests writing these statements down on paper to ensure the mind does not circumvent the process, but the real thing to recognize here is that our suffering is not caused by events or people in our lives. It's all caused by our thoughts, which means we don't have to change anything outside of us to be happy.

How can we bring about the end of war in the world? I'm not afraid to say I don't know for sure. I have experienced periodic states of consciousness that have given me glimpses of the awareness beyond thought that connect us all (awakenings or whatever you want to call that). I now realize that unconditional peace is real, but that our attachment to, and identification with, our thoughts prevent us from experiencing it permanently.

I still have my own set of thoughts and beliefs about the way of the world, but I realize that they are nothing more than thoughts and are potential hindrances to my personal peace. I have seen that my mind is the sole source of conflict in my life, but I still need to remind myself now and then when conflict arises and remain mindful of my thoughts.

Can you create peace in the world without being at peace with yourself? Which is more true, "I can't be at peace unless there is peace in the world," or, "Be peaceful and there will be peace in the world?" It seems to me that making your peace or your happiness contingent on something external makes suffering inevitable, and when we suffer we tend to cause suffering. When we are at peace, we tend to bring about peace. So, go in peace my friend :-)

Chapter 33: Epilepsy and Acceptance

September 26, 2007

My diagnosis with epilepsy in 2004 is what started my original investigation into consciousness, and why I started writing. For the last year and a half, I have been working on getting my driving privileges back, which requires going 6 months without a seizure. Interestingly enough every time I make it 6 months I have another breakthrough seizure, typically in the form of a partial complex as opposed to a grand mal (the partial seizures are much easier to live with but still prevent me from driving). In fact, it has been about a year and a half since my last grand mal.

Having said that, as of Monday night I had been driving for a about a week for the first time in a long time and enjoying being able to take myself places without imposing on anyone. I had just returned home from a Deeksha event (a oneness blessing that I had been to a few times before), parked in the driveway and felt the tell tale signs of an aura starting (auras usually precede a seizure and are like a felt sense that something is about to happen). I made my way upstairs and said hello to my wife, Shelby, but the aura had gotten stronger. She could tell something was not quite right and told me to sit down. It was a very strange sensation compared to past partial seizures and I knew something was not quite right when I started spilling water on the floor, which I did twice before sitting down.

The next thing I really remember was coming to with Shelby on the phone telling someone I had had a seizure. My brother soon showed up and I could sense that they were both worried about me and wanted to take me to the hospital. I was too weak and cloudy headed to communicate with them effectively, but could understand everything they were saying and tried to make it clear that I did not want to go to the hospital. It took me close to an hour before I had regained my ability to communicate effectively and answer questions.

It was during this recovery time that I tried to sit up several times. They were concerned about me getting up and insisted that I remained seated, so I did. I was in somewhat of a forced state of acceptance. Someone wants to put some juice in my mouth. Okay. Someone wants to put essential oil on my temples. Okay. Someone wants to prevent me from standing when I want to stand. Okay. The outcome of acceptance is a much more peaceful state than one of resistance and struggle, especially when those around you are concerned for your well being and doing what they think is best to help. In the end, I had a headache, a little bit of nausea, a sore tongue from biting it, and some fatigue, but I have definitely had worse. What I got in return was a better grasp on the essence of acceptance.

The truth is that we have no control over what happens to us at any given moment. We are totally and always at the mercy of what is, regardless of the lengths to which we go. Any semblance of control is just an illusion. That's why I needed epilepsy in my life – to show me the many facets of acceptance that can't just be read about and understood. One would think the lesson would be obvious since it is a disorder that removes your ability to control your mind and body periodically. But it is just now being fully digested by my analytical brain, or should I say allowed to pass through it.

We experience frustration when what we are experiencing is different from what we think we should be experiencing. No problems exist in a state of acceptance. However, this does not mean you should do nothing to take care of your body. In the case of epilepsy, I have been following the increasing medication route for some time now, and will be exploring the Vegus Nerve Stimulator implant that has helped many other people overcome seizures.

So, you see, I can fully accept my present moment situation and still not resign myself to being stuck in that situation. Rather than hit a wall and try to climb or punch through it, it's like hitting a wall, acknowledging its presence and then searching for a way around it while accepting every part of the wall you encounter on the way.

In all honesty I think my mind was too cloudy to be integrating all of this that night, but it has all made a great deal more sense in retrospect. Epilepsy found me because it was what I needed to see the world for all of the beauty it possesses when I don't impose my beliefs on it. Call me thick headed ;-)

Chapter 34: Navigating the Switch

October 17, 2007

I hope you are doing well and enjoying the transition of the seasons as Fall begins to get situated. A couple of weeks ago, a few days after my last seizure, I had what might be called an awakening experience that lasted most of a day. We were in the car on a beautiful day, my wife was driving and I was just taking in the scenery on a stretch of road that I had seen hundreds of times before. I started to do an eyes open meditation technique I had read about the day before, which included the typical suggestions of relaxing tense muscles, letting go of thoughts as they arise, etc.

After a few moments of this, a strange sensation began to occur. It was the sense of fear, almost like the stage fright you might encounter before making a speech. As it intensified, I felt some tension in my body as well. The sensation was almost like an aura that I might encounter prior to a seizure which only added to the fear of what was happening. Instead of trying to change the mental subject as I have done before when encountering this type of fear, I relaxed and surrendered into it. The message I received while I was on the tipping point was, "You're doing it for humanity," which gave me that final push I needed to fully give in to what was about to happen.

At that point warm tingling sensations began to occur in my body. It grew more intense and felt almost orgasmic in nature. I was overcome with the feeling of joy and exhilaration. It seemed to escalate to a point and then evened out as I took in the beautiful scenery around me, which had suddenly become vivid and alive. I realized that I was seeing everything for the first time ever, and that I was seeing it without a mental story or label attached to it. Everything made perfect sense without the need for thoughts to reconcile it. It was a sense of knowing that settled over me that allowed me to see the beautiful necessity in everything that is happening in the world, including wars and all forms of suffering.

As the full implications of this felt knowing flooded my body, I was on the verge of tears. Not tears of sorrow but tears of joy. Before they started flowing I found myself quietly laughing to myself. It all made perfect sense. I finally got the cosmic joke, "You are what you seek." The truth of who we are is hidden right under our noses, where it's no wonder it gets overlooked.

Though it was beyond what words could describe, it was like seeing how we are all perfectly connected in a way that makes us creators and products all at the same time. I had this sense that we are all pawns in a cosmic conspiracy to bring about this moment, and to see and experience it fully. It occurred to me that everyone with whom we ever come in contact, and even those we don't, regardless of how seemingly insignificant the encounter, are a part of this conspiracy, whether they know it or not. The end goal of the conspiracy is to get us to awaken.

I also realized that everyone I see is actually a reflection of myself. They, too, are the same "thing" I am and the only difference is a perceived difference I've placed on them, which actually says more about me. None of these realizations were in the form of thoughts, as thought seemed to be relatively absent. Instead they were just known or felt. If ever a thought began to form, it was instantly met with a sort of reassurance. For example, I started to wonder if this experience would end and if I would be able to get back to this point if it did, but I was reassured that I did not need to be concerned before the thought had completely formed. It felt as if I was assured that I would be able to return again and again and that this was just a sample. This allowed me to remain present, without worrying about an unknowable future.

Interestingly enough, when my wife asked a question, or if I was in some other way called upon to do something, I seemed to be able to "snap out of it" without losing my connection. My actions also seemed to be much clearer and decisive, without any tension. The sense of joy and wonder remained in the background and available for me to step back into at will. I felt like I was learning to negotiate the switch, so to speak.

On the drive home, I smelled a very potent dead skunk smell. However, before the mind could step in and label it as a "bad" smell it was realized that the only thing that made it a bad smell was past experience. Instead it took on a somewhat sweet smell all its own that was actually rather pleasant (sounds crazy I know).

Throughout the rest of the day, I took great joy in whatever I did, whether it was doing laundry or feeding dogs, watching in wonderment as everything happened of its own accord. I was doing it all for the first time without any stories from days gone by. That night the dinner we ate was among the best I had ever tasted and I was savoring every bite. I had to stop myself from groaning with pleasure as that was a bit much for my fellow diners.

In short, it was a great experience that I savored until I went to bed that night. The next day I woke up to my normal mental activity but with a residue of the pleasure I had encountered the day before. It faded over the course of the next day as I had work to do in preparation for our business trip. Though I have tried on a number of occasions since then to reconnect, I have not had much luck. I have also spent a fair amount of time mentally analyzing the experience knowing that it would not get me back to that point.

I am very fortunate to have experienced that which I've been reading about for the last couple of years and I realize that I am apparently not quite ready to live "it" on a full time basis. I recognize now that "it" is always here and can be experienced by anyone anytime if they are interested. I highly recommend it and look forward to being there (here) again in the near "future." ;-)

Chapter 35: Profoundly Meaningless Words

November 16, 2007

I wanted to take a moment to thank those of you who are reading my writings. Some of you are familiar with the things I write about and have had similar experiences or read similar books, and some of you have no interest whatsoever. Once in a while I'll pick up something from a friend or acquaintance that gives me a clue as to where they are on their particular journey, which often gives me some insight into what they might find valuable.

Just to give you an example, during a recent conversation with a friend who was feeling stressed out, I suggested trying some meditation. She said that she could not meditate unless she was getting a tattoo. She has quite a few and had decided that was the only way for her to relax her mind. I realized during that conversation that there are a large number of people I know who have never tried to meditate at all, or tried unsuccessfully a time or two and dismissed it as something of which they weren't capable.

A day or so after that conversation, a very simple and profound meditation technique came to me. I have used a variation of it before, but just realized how powerful and simple it actually is to convey. I call it the "Blah, Blah, Blah" technique. So, whether you are an old pro at meditation or have never tried it before, I'd like you to take a moment right now to try this. You can either do it with your eyes open or closed, but you might want to do it with your eyes closed if you have never tried to meditate before.

Take a deep breath and relax any muscles that you notice are tense. Then think the words, "Blah.. Blah.. Blah.." (don't say them out loud). Continue to breath in and out through your nose at your own natural pace. Pause a couple of seconds between each "blah" and pause for a few extra seconds after the third "blah." Then repeat, "Blah.. Blah.. Blah.." Be the witness of the thoughts. If it helps, at first you can visualize the words spelled out in front of you as you think them. I also recommend that you pay attention to your body when you do it and relax any muscles you feel tense up.

While doing this, realize that You are not these thoughts. Instead, You are the awareness that "sees" these thoughts. Focus on that part of Yourself that realizes these are just thoughts. You are witnessing these thoughts occur. This creates a space between the thoughts and You. Once that space has been created you can rest with a still mind in that space, noticing any random thought that happens to go through your mind for what it is: a thought.

Take as long as you want to observe the "blahs," but I would recommend spending at least 20 seconds or so. Then spend as long as you want resting in the space of silence you have created (maybe 5 minutes at first). If thinking the words helps you remain in the observer role, then by all means keep thinking them the whole time. Though it may seem silly and pointless at first, you've actually done something quite profound that most people never do. You have broken your identity with thought.

Most of us spend the majority of our waking moments so identified with our thoughts that we don't even realize we are thinking. There's nothing wrong with thinking, but when we are so identified with our thoughts that we lose ourselves in them, we become taken over by the mind (so to speak). By taking a few seconds out of the day a few times a day to do this practice, we break that cycle and connect with ourselves on a much deeper level.

It's a great mental exercise and I recommend you do it when ever you feel stressed, worried, or realize that you are caught in habitual thought. You will likely begin to catch yourself thinking more often during everyday activities, which is a wonderful sign that you are becoming more present. As you begin noticing your habitual thoughts more often, you will probably find that blah, blah, blah actually summarizes most of them nicely.

When you find yourself thinking a thought you would rather not be thinking, don't scold yourself for it, just realize that it is a thought and nothing more. Recognize every unwanted thought as just another "blah." That's all there is to do. In this way, this meditation can be done any time during the day or night without the need for the "blahs" simply by witnessing any thought that happens to be going through your mind.

Feeling Meditation

There is another very simple and powerful technique that helps in day to day life which involves connecting with the body. It too can be done eyes open once you have done it a few times. Start by taking a deep breath and relaxing. Then, try to feel the tip of your finger. With your eyes closed, can you tell if it is still there? When you put your attention on trying to feel it from the inside, you can easily feel the aliveness in it either in the form of your pulse beating in it or even a tingly sensation. Try it now.

Keep your attention here and then put your attention on your whole hand, then both hands. Once you feel the aliveness in your hands, you can focus your attention on your feet, then proceed with other parts of your body until you feel the aliveness running through your whole body. Again, the point is to just spend a little time feeling the aliveness within different parts of your body from time to time throughout your day (without the need for needles being stuck in and out repeatedly). It is very simple and calms the mind dramatically. When you get more accustomed to the practice you can even maintain attention in some part of your body (such as your hands) while talking to someone, driving, or watching TV.

There are obviously hundreds of other ways people use meditation in their daily lives, but these are the two that I have found the easiest to use on a regular basis throughout the day. Connecting with your breathing and following the breath in and out is also a very easy and ancient form of meditation that I started out with a few years ago. However, the goal of all meditation is the same – to break the cycle of habitual thought. We then, can realize for ourselves that we are not our thoughts, which is truly liberating.

Chapter 36: Giving Thanks

November 22, 2007

"Life will give you whatever experience is most helpful for the evolution of your consciousness. How do you know this is the experience you need? Because this is the experience you are having at this moment."

A New Earth, by Eckhart Tolle

There is a conspiracy afoot to bring you to a point where you are experiencing eternal gratitude for everything you encounter. Everyone and everything you encounter is involved, from the person who cut you off in traffic, to the pile of dog poop you stepped in while walking in the park, to the person in the express line with more than twelve items, to the stranger who smiled at you on the street. Their aim is to remind you that all of your suffering is self created through your identification with thoughts. Thoughts are simply electrical impulses that occur in the brain, and what happens in our lives is neither bad nor good until they are interpreted through that neural network of mystery.

All of our emotions are reflections of what we are thinking at the time. Frustration, anger, resentment and fear all happen as a result of our thoughts about a situation, not as a result of the situation itself. This is what our coconspirators are trying to tell us. If we want to be free of negativity, we can learn a great deal from them.

When we treat everyone we come in contact with as a noble messenger who is trying to protect us from our thoughts, we enable the conspiracy to work more effectively rather than fight it. Gratitude is the natural outcome. We then feel like giving thanks to all of those around us who have helped us on our journey, which is ultimately everyone.

Our free will enables us to choose whether to identify with our thoughts and take them to be the absolute truth, or to choose to realize that they are not who we are. Feeling gratitude is our natural state of being when it's not concealed behind a layer of judgments, which is why this time of year is so valuable. It reminds us to set aside trivial matters and connect with that state of gratitude that is in us all. As for me, I am grateful for the role you play in the conspiracy to bring about my realization, and would like to show my thanks by doing the same for you. Happy Thanksgiving :-)

Chapter 37: Tears of Joy

December 9, 2007

A little over a week ago, I experienced something quite beautiful. I went to a satsang (Sanskrit - truth gathering) where a spiritual teacher by the name of Jeannie Zandi (www.jeanniezandi.com) came to share with us her experience of being one with truth. It's rare that I attend such things, in fact this was my first one that involved a live teacher as opposed to a prerecorded one, but I was quite grateful for the opportunity.

We began with a meditation and sat in silence until the last participant arrived (there were nearly 30 of us). As she began speaking I tried to maintain my level of awareness by being focused on the present moment. She spoke for a little while and then began taking questions from the group. There were a few times early on when something was said that resonated so deeply in me that I began to get teary eyed, but I don't remember now the specifics of what was being said.

It was about halfway through or so, when one of the participants started talking about how she knew that everything was beautiful and perfect and so forth, but Jeannie interrupted to tell her to use the first person. Then, the woman began saying things like, "I am beautiful, I am perfect, I am beauty, I am..." While she was talking I finally opened up fully to the fact that she was speaking for me, as well as everyone else in the room. I realized and accepted that she was me, speaking to me, for my benefit, and I began to cry.

The tears kept coming and they kept talking. The man sitting next to me put his hand on my back and told me not to hold back and to be with it, for which I was quite grateful as my mind may have made me uncomfortable had I let it. He and the woman sitting next to him (possibly his wife) provided me with tissue and continuous support. He also told me that it tends to come in waves. This obviously meant that this was not an uncommon experience, but as far as I could tell I was the only one crying uncontrollable tears of joy.

Jeannie did make a comment about it not being a satsang until someone cried, but the questions and answers continued as I cried. I was not judging myself and not experiencing anything other than a beautiful warm and tingly feeling throughout my body. There was no need to analyze or question as everything seemed to make perfect sense. Once in a while my tears would subside a bit, but something else would be said that brought up laughter and more tears. As far as I could tell, I spent the last hour of the meeting crying and laughing at things that were not necessarily funny or sad. It was a surprisingly liberating and beautiful experience.

Toward the end my tears subsided a bit as a man was asking about how we sustain states such as the ones that are experienced during satsang. I knew this was something I too would be curious about if I were not already in a state of joy, plus just pondering such a question seemed a foreign idea at the time. I don't remember exactly what Jeannie's response was now, but it made perfect sense and I think it had to do with him examining who it was that was asking the question (the thinking mind which likes to remain in control, or the Self).

One of the last questions was from a woman who apparently thought that everyone else was experiencing the same level of pain she had, and pointed at me as an example. Apparently she had her own pain and was projecting it on me, assuming I was experiencing tears of sadness. Jeannie was quick to point out that we do not all have the same pain that she was experiencing.

After she finished answering the last question, Jeannie asked the other participants if they would like to check in with me. They expressed interest so she turned to me and asked almost jokingly if I had anything I would like to share with the group about my experience. Then, I began speaking very clearly and easily about my experience, without any nervousness or awkwardness, which I would have ordinarily experienced in such a situation with a room full of strangers. The fear of judgment was oddly absent.

I started by saying jokingly, "She started it," and pointed at the woman (me) who had described herself (me) earlier as beauty, etc. I then explained all I could about the experience and clearly stated that they were not tears of sadness to make sure there were no misunderstandings. After I finished I said, "I hope that lived up to everyone's expectations," and we all had a chuckle.

I was in a very good mood for the next couple of days and found it easy to laugh and easy to tear up with joy when remembering that night. It was also easy for me to see the innate beauty that is all around us, in the trees, the sky, the ground, pretty much everything. As time passed I became more entrenched in my own thoughts about the events around me and thought again became my predominant state of mind.

Though it can be frustrating to experience states such as this and then lose them, it is important not to get attached to a past experience, which may be one of the beneficial lessons to be learned from this. It also points to other things to which we are still attached. The mind likes being in control and likes figuring things out. It's hard for it to accept that it can not understand everything and it will keep trying if you let it. For me, the veil separating me from my Self has been pulled back and then closed a couple of times now, but it does seem a bit thinner. I'll be there once I realize I'm already there, and not a moment before. So will you :-)

Chapter 38: Freedom to Feel

January 17, 2008

I was told recently by a very intuitive aunt-in-law that I was a highly sensitive person deep down and that I had put up barriers for unknown reasons to protect this sensitive core, which has left me somewhat cut off from my feelings. She told me to open myself up to experience these feelings when they arise instead of trying to keep them buried, so that they, too, could experience freedom. This was coming on the heels of me experiencing tears of joy during a satsang I attended, and the conversation struck a chord in me that left me more mindful of my feelings.

What I have noticed is that I have a tendency to avoid feelings as they arise (especially the ones that might cause tears). In the case of hearing about some tragedy in the world or some other story that might cause sorrow, I use my knowing that everything is innately perfect as a reassurance. However, I think there may be an inclination to hide out behind that knowing instead of actually experiencing these feelings to their fullest.

With all of the tragedy going on in the world today, it seems natural for us to avoid negative feelings to a degree, or at least turn off the part of us that might experience it on a personal level. Otherwise, we might get sucked into the endless drama of the world. However, this avoidance can create a disconnect or resistance toward what is.

Since I have been more aware of feelings lately, I have had a few glimpses of this sensitive inner core that I have been protecting. The triggers have come in the form of a moving song, a news story, and meditation just to name a few. When I start to experience the precursor to tears welling up, something akin to fear steps in to prevent it from fully developing. It may be quelled by disguised thoughts like, "I can't just start crying for no reason, so and so will worry or think I'm crazy." But deeper than egoic level fear is a feeling, "I can't open myself that much because it will open me up to a whole new level of vulnerability so great it could kill me." Therein, lies what I think the fear is truly about – the fear of egoic death. Not just the fear of being free to express feelings over seemingly insignificant things, but the fear of being without the ego's protection.

Here is a quote that came back to me recently while scanning through some audio clips on my computer. It's from Adyashanti on a track labeled "What freedom really is."

> "[It is a] myth that [when I'm truly enlightened] I can rest in some assuredness that I will never again feel insecure, or feel fear, or feel doubt, or feel those emotions that we don't want to feel. Forget it. That's not it. That's the pipe dream. That's the opium that's sold to the masses. And they eat it up and they never get there, and they end up disillusioned. That's not how it works. Freedom is never freedom "from." If it's freedom "from" anything, it's not freedom at all. It's freedom "to." Are you free enough to be afraid? Are you free enough to feel insecure? Are you free enough not to know? Are you free enough to know that you can't know? Are you free enough to be totally comfortable, to know that you can't know what's around the next corner? How you will feel about it? How you will respond to it? That you literally can't know? Are you free enough to be totally at ease and comfort with the way things actually are? That's freedom. The other thing is the ego's idea of freedom."
>
> http://www.adyashanti.org/index.php?file=listenonline

Another audio I listened to recently, by Pamela Wilson (http://www.pamelasatsang.com), has several questions from people in the audience regarding how to deal with certain feelings that they considered unpleasant. Pamela likes people to invite those negative feelings into the light of our awareness and find out why they are arising. In one man's case, who was suffering from grief over a lost relationship, their dialogue eventually led to the heart of what that feeling truly was about. Below is paraphrased from the essence of that conversation.

> "Sorrow and love are the same. How could we feel such sorrow if we weren't capable of so much love. Sorrow comes to show us the depths of our love. We are caring itself, and always have been. We are love itself, and always have been. We just didn't realize it. Sorrow just brings love down into the body. It's funny how, in the beginning, emotions obscure who we are, then, later, they can help us realize who we are."
> Pamela Wilson (*Love with Legs* CD: 2005)

Behind every seemingly negative emotion is our true loving self, trying to protect our true loving essence from harm. Whether we are feeling anxiety, frustration, or sadness, when you trace those feelings back to their origin, you will likely find a defensiveness trying to protect you. Fear is often at the center of it, which triggers that defensiveness to step in with a response that has seemingly worked in the past to protect us. Once we see our "negative" feelings for what they truly are we can embrace those feelings as well. We can thank them for trying to protect us. After all, it's happening out of love and for love's sake.

Chapter 39: Love is in the Air

February 10, 2008

I believe that there are as many manifestations of love as there are stars in the sky. Everything we do, we do out of love. We are the walking embodiment of love. Even those actions or feelings that seem on the surface to be linked to pain, anger, sorrow and so on, are nothing more than love being exhibited. Whether it be out of love for ourselves or love for others, it makes no difference. It is one and the same.

When we are grieving the loss of a loved one or the loss of a relationship, it is out of love for that person. When we are angry at someone who has done us wrong, that too is out of love for ourselves and probably that person. When we try to tell someone else how to live, it is out of love for that person. When we fight for what we believe is right, it is out of love for others as well as ourselves. It matters not whether you are at work making money for you and your family who need food to survive, or whether you are at rest indulging in your favorite intoxicant for the love of the feeling it brings with it.

Love is all around us and yet we don't see it unless it is overt. When we see someone taking care of a loved one who is ill or when we see two people looking endearingly at one another, it is more clearly seen as love. Even punishing a child for wrong doing is more clearly an act of love on the surface (unless you are the child).

Even the ego, which tends to view itself as separate from (and often better than) others seems to be just another manifestation of love. The ego wants to be loved by others. It wants to be thought highly of and have its feelings and beliefs honored and respected. It tends to dislike or judge others who do not fit into its strict mold of what is acceptable, or threaten its self image, all in the name of love. In a way, the ego is trying to bring about the desired end result of love through its actions, without realizing its efforts are actually sabotaging its attempts to achieve the end goal. Herein lies the fundamental flaw. We must first realize everything is love before we can experience it as such, and the ego can't help us do that.

To realize all is love and love is all, there must be an effort made to recognize the truth in the statement, "Everything is a manifestation of love." If we hear this statement and make no effort to see the truth in it, then we might make it a belief that allows us to go along doing what we have been doing with a new sense of justification. "Everything I do must be okay because it is just an example of my love for myself or someone else." To do this actually hides the love from yourself and those around you. When love is hidden from view, then what good can it bring?

I invite you to make an effort to bring love out of hiding in everything you do or think. Make love known. When love feels absent, go inside to look for it. When someone says something mean to you, or rubs you the wrong way, don't just react out of habit. Look to see if there is actually a hidden motive tied to love. If our inner core feels threatened or hurt, we tend to react defensively to protect that core. That reaction creates a domino effect of reactivity. But it can be stopped at any time by simply recognizing the underlying motive of love that is being exhibited on both sides.

We're all here to find love. Ironically, it's always here right under our noses. It's as if we are fish swimming in an ocean of love so we don't recognize it for what it is. Instead we focus all of our attention on all of the other fish in the sea who are also blind to the fact that they are living, breathing manifestations of the same thing. Once you see it, you will realize that you have been swallowed up by it all along, and what a wonderful feeling that is. *"All we really want, all we really need is love. love, love. Love is all we need"* - (The Beatles).

Chapter 40: Eliminating Time

March 11, 2008

> "You cannot make the egoless state into a future goal and then work toward it... because it will always seem that you have not arrived yet... Look carefully to find out if your spiritual search is a disguised form of ego. Even trying to get rid of your "self" can be a disguised search for more if the getting rid of your "self" is made into a future goal."
>
> *A New Earth*, by Eckhart Tolle (Page 206)

When reading the quote above under the section on eliminating time, I reread that first paragraph three times, with the full meaning hitting home harder and harder each time, taking me into wakefulness, as if I were watching a movie of my hands holding the book and the print on the page. A sense of joy pervaded me, as well as a little fear of the unknown. I realized that I had indeed made my quest for truth, to be free of ego, into just another obstacle to finding it. I realized that I could never find it if I was in search of it. It's right here. Just step out of time.

Upon later observation I found that I unknowingly spend a great deal of my time thinking about what I'm going to say or do at some point, wondering what to do or say next, what might happen if I do it, what other people (or dogs) think of me, how I'm shaping that image, what's expected of me, why I do these things, etc. I'm frequently unconsciously looking for distractions to avoid being fully present, even if those distractions involve ways to get to the present moment. Lost in thought or doing, but not in what I'm doing right Now. Touching presence periodically but not committing. "Where am I now?" is a question that pulls me back to center when I realize I'm lost in thought.

> "So instead of adding time to yourself, remove time. The elimination of time from your consciousness is the

elimination of ego. It is the only true spiritual practice... What we are speaking of is the elimination of psychological time, which is the egoic mind's endless preoccupation with past and future and its unwillingness to be one with life by living in alignment with the inevitable isness of the present moment."

A New Earth, by Eckhart Tolle (Page 207)

After reading this I stopped and tried to feel what that actually meant. I asked myself, "What would it be like if there was only Now?" Rather than try to answer it with thoughts, I just experienced what life would be like if there was only Now. There is no past. There is no future. No yesterday or tomorrow. Any thoughts that arise regarding either are arising Now. There is not even a five minutes from now. Only Now. I repeated to myself, "There is only Now," as I continued to walk, wash my hands, etc., knowing that each step I was taking was in the Now. Each thing I looked at I was looking at Now. The words I am typing I am typing Now.

Though the full impact of these connections may only be felt for a brief while, it is an exercise that can be done at any time and I highly recommend you give it a try. Feel what it would be like if there was only, ever, Now. Everything else is a figment of your imagination.

At this stage, I can connect with the present moment for short intervals throughout each day, but it is sometimes easier than others. It takes practice, since we have been identified with our thoughts for so many years, but it does get easier with practice. The key is not to get frustrated when it seems hard to do.

I've been trying to take mental notes on what makes it easier for me and those mental notes are typically what take me out of the Now. So it is a bit of a double edged sword, but one that I hope will allow me to share with others some techniques that might help them connect with the Now.

It is helpful when thoughts come to stop and ask, "Where am I?" rather than getting caught up in the story. I stay with it for as long as

I can and just enjoy the feeling while it lasts. Distractions ultimately pop up that take away attention, but the more often we can do that, the easier it gets.

Another thing that helps is to focus all of my attention on every step I take while going to the kitchen, walking across a room, pouring a glass of water, etc. I may not feel the same warm and tingly feeling I often get from other experiences of the present moment, but it is still a state of limited or no thought. When you are present in what you are doing, you are not focused on the future or past. Every little bit helps and makes it easier. There is only Now. Just immerse yourself in it.

Chapter 41: Miscellaneous Quotes, Realizations and Meditations

March 26, 2008

Below are some things that have come my way that I have written down over the last few months. They serve as helpful reminders for me and I felt the need to share them with you in case they might be beneficial to you in your life. Feel free to share with others. I hope you enjoy.

"As soon as you learn how to treat your wife [significant other] with respect, you will have a much better life." by Shelby Carland.

My wife is always good at pointing out when I am reacting out of habitual programming and not from a place of truth or compassion. Her gentle reminders help me realize when I am neither being present nor mindful in my interactions. Our significant others can be very valuable teachers when it comes to recognizing our own ego.

"There's no better song in the world than the one you are listening to right now." Note to Self

This one came to me one evening while listening to the radio and a song that moved me came on. I hadn't heard it before, but I allowed myself to open up as I listened. The message hit home with a great deal of energy but I realized that all songs can be just as powerful if we allow ourselves to listen to them without judgement, as if it is the first time we had ever heard music before. Each note disappearing forever as it is replaced by a new one.

"Give EVERYTHING you do your fullest attention." Note to Self

When I realized how being fully present could be maintained in daily life, it became clearly summarized by these words. If you are giving what you are doing your full attention, there is no room for dwelling on the past or future. In fact, there is very little room for mental noise at all. Stillness and the significance of each simple thing captures the attention.

"My ego makes me do things I don't want to do, and prevents me from doing things I want to do." Note to Self

One day, while I was paying attention to the thoughts going on in my head, I realized that I had stopped myself from doing something for fear of what someone might think. I've noticed that this is fairly common for me and feel grateful when I notice it. On the flip side of the coin, when I am identified with my ego (possessed by it is more like it), I do or say things that I did not want to do or say. The ego is on autopilot and just doing what it has done for years without my knowing. This is also nice to catch even if it is not caught until after the fact. Noticing is all it takes to be free of the ego's control over us.

"Is there resentment in the action you're doing right now? Did you know there doesn't need to be? Forgiveness can save the whole world from self destructing, but only if enough people participate. No one else will forgive unless you do it first and continue to do it for the rest of your life. Once you take the first step, nothing else will matter." Note to Self

This one came to me one morning when I was awakened by one of our dogs needing out to pee. It was probably 4:00 or 5:00 a.m. and I reluctantly got up to walk them. As I was headed to the back door I realized that I was carrying resentment with me over having to do this on multiple occasions. I realized that my mind had created a mental story painting me as the victim. I was using the past to illustrate the unfairness of life (one of the ego's favorite past times). I realized at that point that having resentment was a choice and I chose not to engage in it. I became present and wiped my mind clear of past, as if this was the first time I had ever walked the dogs before dawn. What a blessing it turned out to be. I got to see the morning star, in all its brilliance, illuminating the woods around me. The predawn sky was just beginning to lighten and I felt honored to have seen something I would not have seen had it not been for the seeming inconvenience of being "awakened" from my sleep. I have since come to accept the role of early morning dog walker and try to use it as a way to see what it is I'm missing.

> "True freedom and the end of suffering is living in such a way as if you had completely chosen whatever you feel or experience at this moment."
>
> *Stillness Speaks*, by Eckhart Tolle

I had to mention this Eckhart quote because it, so beautifully, sums up overcoming our ego identification. Why would there be any resentment if I chose this moment to be as it is? Why would there be any negative emotions at all? I have seen enough to feel that everything happens for a reason, which means that everything that comes my way does so for a reason far bigger than the mind can comprehend. Though we have no control over what happens in life and are at life's mercy, we can choose how we feel about everything life throws at us. When it came to the resentment I had over dog walking, I realized I had a choice and I chose to accept what life had given me, which turned out to be a beautiful sky. Acceptance of what is, is another way to sum it all up.

"The future is unknowable. The past is memory. The present is real." Note to Self

Since I find myself spending time in the "what if" land of an imaginary future or dwelling on the memories of things that have already happened, I occasionally realize that these are just thoughts that are happening now. If I'm identified with my thoughts and don't realize I'm thinking them, I am actually reliving the past or acting as if the future has already come. This makes these imaginary realms seem real. When I catch this, I realize that there is only now and that the past has no power over me and the future only needs to be used for planning certain activities and not constantly throughout the day.

Notes to Self

When you are able to step fully into the present, you can stop to smell the roses and truly appreciate the life that is all around.

Meditations

The following are meditation exercises that I wrote down to help remind me of how I can connect with the present moment more easily. I've been trying to take mental notes on what makes it easier for me to become present, which means losing the present moment awareness to a certain extent. But it's worth it if someone else can benefit. I call them Familiar Surroundings I and Familiar Surroundings II but they are interwoven.

Familiar Surroundings I

View the world as if it's the first time you've ever seen it. Pretend you're a visitor to a place you've never seen before and get in the mind set of trying to take it all in as if it's completely new and fascinating. Be in awe of everything around you, without judging it or getting caught up in the story behind it all. Then, do that in everything you do from going to the refrigerator to get something to eat or drink, to walking down the hall or street. Start doing it with all of your routine activities and it will breathe new life into everything you do. You will start to see the truth in it all.

Familiar Surroundings II

Look out a window or stand outside looking at some trees, or the forest, or whatever happens to be in the surrounding area. Then ask yourself, "What if I had never seen this before and this was the first time in my life I had ever laid eyes on this? What would it look like to eyes that had never seen such a thing?" Then look around at everything in that context, as if it were all totally new to you. Allow a sense of awe and wonderment to fill your body over the miracle that you are witnessing. Let that sweep over your body and fill you with warmth. If thoughts arise, be the witness of those thoughts and don't follow them. Let them fall by the way side and continue to focus on the totally new and foreign sites you see as you look around. It may be helpful, if thoughts come, to stop and ask yourself, "Where am I?" Stay with it for as long as you can and just enjoy the feeling while it lasts.

Distractions ultimately pop up that take away our attention, but the more times you can step out of time, the easier it gets. You may not feel the same warm and tingly feeling every time, but you are, none the less, in a state of limited or no thought. You are present in what you are doing and not focused on the future or past.

The last exercise I will leave you with is a popular form of self inquiry that has been suggested by many different spiritual teachers. It too can have a profound impact on connecting with who you truly are. We'll call it the Who Am I exercise.

Right now, sitting where you are, reading these words, take a few moments to breathe deeply and feel your body. Settle yourself... relax... come fully into this moment. Close your eyes for a moment if you need to, then proceed. As you look at the print on this page, ask yourself, "Who is here seeing these words?" Rather than searching for an answer with your mind, shift your attention to what is behind your eyes looking out of them. Ask yourself, "Who am I?" If thoughts arise, notice them and ask, "Who has these thoughts?" "Who is the thinker of these thoughts?" Let thoughts fall away as you continue to look for who is behind them. Continue to ask questions and look deeper within. "What is it that sees these words?" "Who is looking through my eyes?" Feel for the answer. Turn your awareness inward and direct it at the one who sees. Look within to see who sees. Ask yourself, "Who am I?" on a regular basis and don't try to find an answer, just experience what it's like to connect with who you are.

Chapter 42: Moving Sidewalk of Life

April 21, 2008

"Keep your focus peripheral as you look out from this inner cave, from this sweetness. Let your eyes, instead of actively looking out at the world, simply receive the world. Instead of putting your public face on, let innocence be there, let openness be there, let the world come right inside to you without moving a muscle to try and manage it. Openness itself sitting in a chair, daring to not have a strategy about how to get through the next moment, just openly here and receiving."

Jeannie Zandi

We were recently staying at a hotel which had some elaborate decor. One day while riding the escalator up to the second floor, I decided to take a moment to be present, after all I was being propelled toward my destination without effort and could just take a moment to absorb what was around me. I looked into the huge chandelier that hung from the ceiling next to the escalator and allowed myself to look at it from the perspective of the observer that lives within my body, and yet has never seen anything before because all it knows is the present moment. A warm and tingly feeling came over me as my awareness shifted to that of a peripheral one in which I became aware of everything in my peripheral vision as well as what was right in front of me. In effect, my awareness grew to the point where it seemed almost like an out of body experience in that I was not attached to my body, I was the witness of it and all that was around it (hearing, seeing, and smelling it all).

I experienced this several times while at the hotel and it seemed to just take a simple shift in awareness or point of view, from person to observer. Most of the time I did it when I was alone such as when I went to the bathroom or was walking alone or riding elevators, etc.

I like the metaphor of the escalator because it seems to be an accurate description of our lives. To a certain extent we are at the mercy of where we are taken and what appears in our field of awareness.

It was during these moments that the teachings and techniques I have learned about all made sense – Present moment awareness is the key. We are the witness or observer of thoughts, and not our thoughts. Thoughts conceal the fact that we are consciousness or awareness itself. – But I saw them for what they are – pointers that do not accurately describe the truth. The truth can only be experienced.

I often ran into the ego during these brief moments. It was seen from a new perspective of clarity, though it's hard to put into words. It was seen clearly that ego was an obstacle to this present moment experience and could easily hide it (and usually does). I understood that the present moment was always right here, under the surface of our identification with thought, and thoughts had to be still to see it (or were stilled by allowing myself to see it). Breathing, inner body awareness, and relaxation were seen for their importance as this experience can cause some bodily tension and "stuff" to come up.

The basic experience was one of peace, realization, as well as compassion for those who had not discovered what is always here but so rarely seen. I got the sense that there are different depths to the experience, but I never spent long diving deeper. It took making a conscious choice to see and I did not choose it for long periods. Instead I practiced connecting for brief moments and occasionally while I was in the presence of others, trying to give them my full awareness (a bit more difficult). Sometimes it seems easier to become fully present than others, so I hope to continue this practice and deepen it when the opportunity allows.

I'll leave you with the following quote that serves as yet another useful pointer toward the ever present moment.

Notes to Self

"Now is the time to have a direct introduction to this moment. This moment is free of time, of mind, of any notions...introduce yourself to this moment."

Papaji (http://www.avadhuta.com)

Chapter 43: It's Okay to Love

April 21, 2008

We recently were faced with the tough decision many pet owners face in their lives – having a beloved pet put down. It was tougher than usual because our Boxer girl, Lotus, was still alert and at times energetic. But she just would not eat. She had been fasting off and on for close to a month, despite all of the various home cooked combinations and appetite stimulants we tried. Since she had become so thin and was eating just barely enough to stay alive we decided the time had come and that she was not going to make it much longer.

It was difficult on many levels, as many of you already know. But I learned something very valuable from it all. At one point, about a week before we actually had her put down, I was sitting with her on the couch petting her and crying as if it were her last night with us. It occurred to me as my tears fell on her that I was mourning a dog who had not died yet and that I was living in the future. It's inevitable that we are all going to die and it could happen at any time. But we don't spend our lives mourning about the death of a loved one who hasn't died yet, or even our own death for that matter. This realization helped me come back to the present moment and just shower her with love, enjoying the fact that I was spending quality time with her Now.

After my first dog died as a young boy, I took it hard and a part of me closed up and became reluctant to love for fear of the inevitable pain I might feel if the object of my love were taken away, by death or some other means. I didn't really want to have dogs around after that because I knew I would likely outlive them and have to go through the pain of losing them. But, as it would turn out, I ended up with a dog lover of a wife, and a lot of dogs over the years. They have always been in my life trying to teach me things, including some things I did not want to face, one of which was my fear of becoming overtly attached. This was sort of a self preservation measure that kept me from loving as deeply as I could, or at least demonstrating openly how deeply I cared.

Around the time Lotus began her decline, a friend of mine reassured me that it's okay to love, and reminded me that our true essence is love. But it was not solidified in me until the day we had Lotus put down. That day the lesson hit home – it's okay to love. There may be grief when the physical form of who we love disappears, but their essence never leaves us. They remain a part of who we are. The grief we experience is yet another form of love, and though the grief passes, the love never does.

From my experience you can either allow the death of a loved one to harden your heart and make you bitter, or you can realize that death is inevitable. Life is short so don't make your life miserable about something that hasn't happened yet or happened in the past. Enjoy it while you have it. I take comfort in the idea that nothing really ever dies, it just changes forms.

Chapter 44: The Circle of Life - Revisiting Recurrent Themes

May 31, 2008

Over the past few years of truth seeking, I have been sharing my experiences along the way with all of my friends and family in the hopes that my search would be contagious. After reading multiple books from multiple teachers, I have been led to the point where all of the paths converge. This is my attempt to encapsulate all that I have learned, so I apologize in advance for the repetition. I will say that I've always found repetition of the same simple truths, discussed differently, to be very beneficial for integration.

The present moment is all there ever really is. Life is always unfolding right Now. The situations that arise in life are completely out of our control, which can be frustrating and even painful, but it is not the situations that cause us pain. It is our thoughts about them. Events and situations can be blamed and resisted, but it does not change the fact that they are here now. This is where acceptance comes into play. If one is to be truly happy, the acceptance of what is, is a crucial element. It seems so simple really. If you want to live a life of joy, simply love what is, in this moment. Feel free to take steps to change it, but acknowledge its necessity first.

Our beliefs are at the center of all of our negative emotions. When we encounter something that causes discomfort, we believe that what's happening should not be happening. Beliefs are simply thought patterns we have picked up along the way that we use to judge the world around us. As I once read, if you think something is a fact rather than a belief, ask yourself if there is one person in the world who would disagree with that "fact." If the answer is yes, then it is a belief and not a fact. When we believe situations should be a certain way, disappointment and pain are inevitable because things will not always fit our beliefs about how they should be.

Another facet of the human experience has to do with our personal identity. We are actually not who we think we are. We are

117

so identified with our thoughts that we rarely see what lies beneath. That which lies prior to, or underneath, thought is often referred to as awareness or consciousness. That is what we are. It is ever present but our thoughts cover up its existence because awareness is totally identified with thought most of the time. Connecting with the awareness that we all are is truly liberating, and we can connect with it anytime we so choose.

There are numerous ways to connect with who we truly are, and I've included a few pointers below that have been working consistently for me. I have found that some techniques "work better" at certain times than others, so a bit of experimentation may be helpful.

Focus all of your attention on what you are doing Now. Give each activity, regardless of how insignificant, your fullest attention.

Focus your attention on your inner body. Feel what it feels like to feel your body. Become aware of the force that animates your body and how it feels to abide in this body. You are not the body, but you do seem to inhabit it. What does it feel like to be an unbiased inhabitant of a living, breathing, sensing being?

Accept what occurs each moment without resistance. If the situation calls for you to take action your action will come from a space of acceptance and will be a much more "level headed" and effective response to any given situation. Realize that what is going on now is exactly what "should" be happening. The universe is giving us just what we need to grow even if it doesn't seem like it on the surface. Is there a hidden gift or silver lining to a seemingly negative situation?

Ask yourself, "Who am I?" Don't look for an answer to the question. Simply focus your attention inward. Ask yourself repeatedly and "look" behind the question to see who it is that is asking the question. Who is it that is aware of the question being asked?

What all of the above practices have in common is that they stop the incessant stream of thoughts that pervade our everyday lives. That allows awareness to become aware of itself, and gives awareness space to act through us. This is a very powerful experience, but don't create any preconceived notions about what it "should" be like. Don't even do it with the intention of "getting" something out of it. These are the crafty thought patterns that can distract you from experiencing that which you truly are. Don't judge the situation to see if you are doing it right, just know that you can't do it wrong.

One of the e-books I read recently (which is available for free at the link below) provides a clear understanding of the self inquiry method mentioned above. The book is called M*eeting Ramana Maharshi* by John Sherman. John is an ex-bank robber turned spiritual teacher and does an excellent job of putting Ramana's teachings of self inquiry into perspective.

http://www.riverganga.org

After reading it, I began to practice focusing my awareness on the awareness that I am. It is simply a shift in perspective that is so obvious it gets overlooked, which is why it is often referred to as the cosmic joke. We've always been aware. Our undeniable awareness has been under our noses all along. So simple, but so oddly difficult to notice.

In my experience, turning attention inward makes the world come alive. The colors and textures become much more vivid. Thought subsides and I am able to just Be (see my previous post on *The Moving Sidewalk of Life*). As John says, this inquiry is self realization and if you continue to practice it, you will eventually no longer need to practice. It will become your normal state of being.

If you are interested in finding out who you truly are and freeing yourself from all forms of suffering, all it takes is your strong intention to do so and you will succeed. I highly recommend downloading the free e-book mentioned above and start practicing turning your attention inward as often as possible. Incorporating daily meditation into your routine is extremely valuable, regardless of how much time you take. Meditation can then become a part of your everyday life as you walk around doing your daily activities. Just direct your attention inward whenever you happen to think of it.

I wish you the very best in all that you do and am grateful that you took the time to read this. May it benefit you in some way. Wishing you eternal peace and love. After all, that's what you already are even if you haven't noticed yet :-)

Chapter 45: Memories

June 14, 2008

I know by now you are quite familiar with the idea that the present moment is all there ever is, has been, or ever will be, but I wanted to use memories as an example of how one can touch that which is always present. Think back to your earliest memory. Visualize it as if you are reliving it. For me this was when I was two years old. My mom was going into the hospital to give birth to my brother. I was in the car with my uncle Bill and I had a can of peanuts between my legs. As we were pulling away, I spilled the peanuts between my legs. As I was trying to pull them out from under me, I realized that they had slid so far up under me that I couldn't reach them. So I lifted my butt up and as I did the peanuts went sliding back under the seat and into the floorboard (the back of the seat had a gap where it met the bottom seat). I also remember my uncle being a bit flustered by this.

When I think back on this memory, I look at what has not changed since then. The one who witnessed it all happen is the same one who is witnessing these words being typed on a screen. It is the same "I" that has witnessed all of my life situations and will continue to witness all of my life situations. It has not changed throughout my entire life. My physical body has changed, my thoughts and ideas have changed, my likes and dislikes have changed, but that "I" that has witnessed it all has not changed. This is the ever-present awareness that we truly are. Everything we experience happens in the space of that awareness, which untouched by the mental interpretations of those experiences. The mind labels, judges and learns from these experiences, but the awareness behind it all has no stake in the outcome. It is simply here.

When you look back on any of your past experiences, you are "seeing" them Now from that same awareness that was seeing them then. Focusing your attention on that awareness is how you can "see" that which you really are, underneath the thoughts and mental labels. Asking yourself, "Who am I?" or "Who is this "I" that is witnessing all of these things happen (past or present)?" is a very effective way of turning your awareness back on itself, or becoming aware of awareness.

Once you have become aware of your own awareness, you can then look at others with that awareness and see them as that same awareness. They may look and act differently, have different life experiences, but deep down they are nothing more than that same pure awareness. You can, in effect, look through the eyes of another and see that there is a background of awareness behind everything they say, do and see.

It's from this space of recognizing all as awareness where true compassion arises. Ultimately there is no difference between me and you. We are all just conscious awareness. This is what all of the spiritual teachings are pointing toward. They all provide pointers to going beyond thought so that we can view the world as this awareness, and, in so doing, become that which we already are. Interacting with life situations from that space is how we can achieve a state of peace. A peace that most of us have only briefly glimpsed in our lives.

There are many practices that assist in disassociating with thoughts so that we can rest in that spacious awareness, but one of the most simple (other than self inquiry) is one that is mentioned in *The Power of Now* by Eckhart Tolle. Ask yourself, "I wonder what I am going to think next?" Then focus your attention and wait for a thought to occur as if you were a cat intensely watching a mouse hole. When a thought occurs, let it go and ask the question again. Then go back to waiting for the next thought. While in that state of waiting, without thought, you are completely present as that awareness.

There are many other portals to connecting with awareness and I recommend you try them all. Don't just try them once. Engage in them on a regular basis throughout your day. It will become easier and easier to go deeper into self awareness. Just be still and see what happens.

Chapter 46: When to Act vs. When to Accept

June 29, 2008

One of the gray areas for many of us in search of happiness involves acting on vs. accepting what is in our interpersonal relationships. I would like to share with you my own experiences with this, as well as what I have read.

As an example, when I am engaged in a conversation with someone and they say something about me that I feel is untrue, I try to accept that rather than react to it. In fact, I go a step further to look for the truth in what is being said to or about me. Other people tend to point out the things in us that we don't want to deal with, or haven't dealt with yet, especially if what they are saying causes an emotional reaction in us (that's important to be aware of).

Even if you know what they are saying about you is untrue, it is true for them at that moment. Sometimes I can see clearly how another person is actually projecting their own issues onto me, but I usually don't point that out to them as it may not be well received. I also try to look for the truth in what they are saying before dismissing it as their own projection so as not to miss an unresolved issue in myself. The main thing I try to do is notice when I feel "wronged" in some way, and respect the other person for where they are on their journey. I don't try to convince them they are wrong, or paint myself as some sort of victim.

The reality of this moment is what is being presented to us, regardless of what form that takes. As Byron Katie points out, "When I argue with reality, I lose – but only 100% of the time." So rather than argue with reality when I don't like what it has presented, I try to make peace with it and take action from that space. I remember that we are always being presented with exactly what we need at this moment, otherwise it would not be happening. I try to look at my life situation as if it is calling me to awaken. Life serves as my mirror. My ideas about myself are projected out onto others and I can learn from that, if I am open and not in a state of resistance.

It's also been illustrated to me that when someone takes their pain out on me in the form of anger or hostility, it ultimately has nothing to do with me. It has to do with their own past pain and suffering. This makes it much easier for me not to take things personally, or at least notice when I do. If someone seems angry at me, I know deep down that I am playing an important role in bringing something to that person's attention that they have not dealt with yet, just as they are doing for me. I am just a mirror of them and vice versa, so I look at it from that perspective. Regardless of whether we are acting consciously or unconsciously, we are all part of a universal process designed to bring about freedom in one another, whether we like it or not, accept it or resist it.

When someone close to me is suffering and I want to help but don't know what to do, I can accept my "not knowing" as it is. In so doing, I have had ideas come to me out of that state of accepting my own confusion. In effect, clarity can come from a state of confusion when we surrender to the fact that we don't have a clue what to do. Meditation can also aid in finding the "right" action by becoming fully present and putting out an intention or question. It's said that we can not ask a question we don't already know the answer to, which I have found to be true. That means we just need to clear our minds so that answer can come to us.

At this stage, I am constantly seeing how identification with the past creates hostility and suffering in myself and other people. When I see two people arguing or saying things designed to hurt, or complaining about something someone said to them, I see how simple it would be for them to release that feeling, simply by doing The Work (as Byron Katie refers to it) on the issues at hand, or by becoming fully present with no concept of an imagined past.

It is not the other person causing the suffering we experience, it's our own thoughts about the situation or person. I typically don't offer this up to people because they may not want to rid themselves of those negative feelings. Ridding ourselves of negativity may mean giving up our victim identity or having to admit we might be wrong. That's a scary concept for the ego.

The conclusion I have come to is to accept, then act if need be. If I can't accept something, I look within to see what is causing the resistance. It always has to do with me and not someone else. Once my present situation is accepted fully, I can then act more efficiently than when I am in resistance. Resistance just creates more resistance in the mirror of the world we are looking at, so it's up to me (and you) to make the world a better place.

Below are some quotes from *Loving What Is* by Byron Katie, I think you will enjoy.

If [he] says something that hurts, he's just revealed what you haven't wanted to look at yet. The man is a Buddha. (Page 133)

[W]e're babies just learning how to live out our love. We keep trying to meet love in everything and everyone, because we haven't noticed that we already have it, that we ARE it. (Page 261)

What I love most about reality is that it's always the story of a past. And what I love most about the past is that it's over. (Page 269)

"It's a tree. It's a table. It's a chair." Is it true? Have you stopped to ask yourself? Have you ever become still and listened as you asked you? Who told you it was a tree? Who was the original authority? How did they know? My entire life, my entire identity, had been built on the trust and un-inquiring innocence of a child. (Page 300)

But even the Now is a concept. Even as the thought completes itself, it's gone, with no proof that it ever existed, other than as a concept that would lead you to believe it existed, and now that one is gone too. Reality is always the story of a past. Before you can grasp it, it's gone. Each of us already has the peaceful mind that we seek. (Page 303)

We [the world around you] don't know how to change; we don't know how to forgive or how to be honest. We're waiting for an example. You're the one. You are your only hope, because we're not changing until you do. Our job is to keep coming at you, as hard as we can, with everything that angers, upsets, or repulses you, until you understand. We love you that much, whether we're aware of it or not. The whole world is about you. (Page 310)

Chapter 47: Driving Lessons

July 22, 2008

Three and a half years after being diagnosed with epilepsy and losing my driving privileges, I am now back in the driver's seat. It was so beneficial for me to be relegated to the passenger seat all of these years, and I am just now realizing the significance of it all. It helped teach me surrender and acceptance of not being in control. I've ridden with many different people with different driving styles over the years and have had to put my faith in each one to get me from point A to B in one piece.

I wouldn't say that I made a "good" passenger necessarily. There were countless times, while riding with my wife (who is a very good driver, by the way), that I over reacted to situations by grabbing the "oh shit" handle. That tended to stress her out even more and it showed my lack of trust in her abilities. But I occasionally found myself preparing for what I thought would be certain impact. In effect, I was reacting to a future possibility that never happened (except for that one time when she did slam into the back of a car that stopped suddenly, but that's another story). I gradually improved in my ability to remain present and allow it all to be.

Now that I am back behind the wheel, I'm learning a great deal more about what driving is really about. I have been a bit more inconsistent than I used to be, sometimes going under the speed limit and sometimes over, always knowing that I'm going the right speed. I'm just taking in the scenery from a whole new perspective. My wife, who is now having to adjust to passenger life with someone who doesn't drive the way she does, sometimes points out that I am driving too slow or too fast. I've had a few good laughs over her comparing me to a 90 year old driver.

But one of the things I've noticed from this is that if I believe the thought that I am doing it wrong, I create stress for myself. It's not her comments about my driving, it's my reaction to them that does that. I love that. I can be a stress free driver if I so choose.

However, there is this whole other side of driving that I am rediscovering. Bad drivers used to be one of my pet peeves when I was behind the wheel. I lost that pet peeve as a passenger because it wasn't my problem to deal with anymore, which gave me the ability to see the hidden lessons for those who were impacted by poor driving. Now I'm getting to see my old reactive patterns resurface. I see how easy it is for me to project onto other drivers.

For example, if I'm going the speed limit and someone behind me is following closely, I project that they are in a hurry and I am slowing them down. I can't know that for sure, but when I believe that thought, it creates tension in me. I notice a tendency to always be checking in with the surrounding cars and projecting how my driving is impacting their view of me. I notice tension in my right thigh, which has so much "riding" on it. (On a side note, I had a lot of body work done a few months back and discovered a great deal of pent up emotional energy in my right thigh).

Also, when I get in a situation where I accidently cut off someone in traffic (it's happened a time or two), I can create a whole story for the other person on how they might be angered by what I have done. I notice my tendency to justify my actions, possibly even blaming them. I can monitor them in my rearview, looking for evidence to support my belief about how they must be feeling. When I see that happen I realize that I am, again, the cause of my own stress. I'm seeing how I concoct stories about the drivers around me and how I'm affected by seeing them as stories instead of just other people going from point A to B, going through the same things I'm going through. What a wonderful lesson it has been to see driving without the stories.

Driving can be such a relaxing meditation when I don't allow myself to believe the stories I create. I can give my full attention to the beautiful scenery, the road ahead, and allow myself to relax, knowing that whatever will be will be. I'm being propelled through space, not knowing what the next moment will bring, without the stress of how I will react to it. Even though I'm the one driving, I'm

N

not in control in any way. But that's another observation in and of itself. May you drive safely and without stories.

Chapter 48: Out of Control

August 1, 2008

One of the recurring themes in my readings and self inquiry lately has pointed me toward the idea that we are immersed in a continuous unfolding of events over which we have no control. I'm noticing more and more that as things happen in our lives, we impose thoughts on these happenings that make us think that we are somehow responsible for their occurrence. But in reality we can not know for sure that we are actually responsible. It has been said many times by many different people that we are not the "doer." Our mind tells us that we are doing these things and can readily show us evidence of how true that is. But if you allow yourself to look deep enough to see the fallacy in that belief, you may get a glimpse of the freedom that can be experienced without that belief.

Byron Katie has this to say: "I invite everyone to notice where their hands are right now. Where their feet are right now and did you put them there? Did you plan it or was it a happening? You know, it could be that we are being done and everything else is just a story we're believing and who would you be without your story? Not forever, but just right here, right now, in this moment, who would you be without your story?"

Our mind takes credit for what we do and is uncomfortable with the idea that we are not the controller of our lives. Our mind thinks that it is doing things on its own, and getting things done. The mind creates stories about what it does that reinforce the illusion that the "it" doing things is the "me" I see myself as.

Jeannie Zandi poses these questions: "What if everything is always happening through you; not yours, not something you created? But is being created through you? What if it's not up to you? What if it's not even a little up to you?"

Eckhart Tolle points out that we are not the thinker. Instead we are being thought. In fact, our thoughts are not personal and have nothing to do with who we really are. They just arise and then disappear. When we believe them, we see ourselves as separate entities rather than the animating force behind our thoughts. His suggestion is to not take our thoughts all that seriously. Tolle also suggests that you can "choose" to step out of identification with the mind and into presence. But what is really happening when you choose to be present, is that presence is choosing to emerge. It appears that the little "me" is choosing it, but it is happening by itself. He suggests that it is helpful to think that you are making it happen even though it is happening by itself through you.

Katie also has this to say, "Being present means living without control and always having your needs met. For people who are tired of the pain, nothing could be worse than trying to control what can't be controlled. If you want real control, drop the illusion of control. Let life live you. It does anyway."

I invite you to visualize what it would be like if you had no control over your life, nor where it is taking you. Visualize what it would be like to know that everything that needed to be done would be done, and right on time. What would it be like if every decision that needed to be made would be made through you and would be made in your best interest? I invite you to go deeply into what life would be like with the confidence that you are like a puppet being guided through life by a force that knows what is in your best interest, where making a mistake is impossible. Observe that force in action as it breathes you, feeds you, walks you down the sidewalk, or drives you down the road. What does that experience look like for you?

For me it looks like total freedom. Total inner peace and acceptance of what is become the norm. From that place I could go about life following it wherever it decided to take me, without worry or stress or conflict, with a deep knowing that whatever happened was exactly what I needed. I wouldn't become complacent, or worry about complacency, because something wants to experience this life to its fullest through me.

Michael Gazzaniga, a prominent neuroscientist, has this to say, "The left brain weaves its story in order to convince itself and you that it is in full control... What is so adaptive about having what amounts to a spin doctor in the left brain? The interpreter is really trying to keep our personal story together. To do that, we have to learn to lie to ourselves." (From *Loving What Is*, by Byron Katie - Introduction)

Here is another quote from an interview with Byron Katie: "You know what I love about this world? No control. No control. Oh my goodness! What could be better than that? We are not the doer. We can just watch." But when we believe the thoughts that say we are in control, and things don't go our way, we become frustrated. When a thought arises, and we see that thought as just another happening, we don't use it to delude ourselves into thinking we are the doer.

There is quote after quote I could share with you from various sources. Instead I just invite you to entertain the possibility that we are "being done" rather than "doing the doing." To do so makes surrender so much easier, and surrendering to what is, is the ultimate key to peace.

When I asked Jeannie Zandi about how free will fits into the grand scheme of things, she said, "We must function with a full intentioned heart and at the same time with a sense of the futility of changing anything without the will of God. Basically that's what we surrender to - the Holy Will - and what we surrender is our own will."

Katie puts it like this, "When you no longer have a will of your own, there is no time and space. It all becomes a flow. You don't decide, you flow from one happening to the next, and everything is decided for you."

Enjoy the ride. You can't do it wrong :-)

[Byron Katie quotes are from an interview with Bill Harris, *Mastering Eckhart Tolle's the Power of Now - A Conversation with Byron Katie.* Available at:
http://rozwojosobisty.files.wordpress.com/2008/08/byron_katie.pdf
http://www.scribd.com/doc/45885516/BYRON-KATIE]

Chapter 49: We Only Hurt the Ones We Love

September 19, 2008

About a month or so ago, I was at the DMV getting my driver's license renewed. Not surprisingly there was a fairly long wait. I was sitting there, observing my surroundings and meditating a bit. A man and woman came in and sat down across from me with their son (maybe 4 or 5 years old). The boy was interested in exploring a bit, but not straying far from his parents. The father decided the boy should be sitting in a chair next to him rather than wandering about. After the boy was placed in his chair, he got bored and got up to stand in front of his chair. The father gently popped his behind and told him to sit down. The boy really didn't want to, so the father decided it was time for some disciplinary action because the boy was not obeying. So the man took the boy by the arm and walked him down a hallway to spank him. The boy knew what was coming and started to cry, causing much more disturbance than the boy was causing before.

When they came back the boy was sniffling a bit and the father placed him in the chair next to him. The boy got up and wanted to go sit on the other side next to his mother. The father was insistent that the boy sit next to him (the mother was reading something and not getting involved). When the boy went to sit next to his mother, against his father's wishes, the man took the boy again by the arm down the hall. This time the boy was crying much louder than before and trying to pull away. He said through his tears, "I just want to be good." Despite the boy's plea, the father proceeded to take him down the hall and discipline him. It was very heartbreaking and frustrating to watch.

When they came back, the boy went over and sat by his mother, which was allowed this time. Meanwhile, I was grappling with my own emotions over what I had witnessed. I felt extreme compassion for the little boy who was just trying to be good. But I was having problems having compassion for the father. I thought about how this man was probably raised the same way and was under the impression this was the best way to raise a child. I thought about how this child's karmic disposition may have placed him in this situation to somehow shape his life in unimaginably positive ways. I thought about the mother who stayed out of it the whole time, wondering if she had been taught by her husband not to get involved.

Despite all of these attempts to rationalize my way into feeling compassion, I was still feeling anger toward the man. I tried doing The Work in my mind which led me to remember something Byron Katie said in one of her books. She was asked how she would react if she saw a mother in a store abusing her children in some way. Katie said that she would see that and remember a time when she too felt that way, angry and confused at her children, lashing out at them. She said she might approach the woman with a deep compassion and ask if she could help, or even tell the woman that she, too, had been in her situation and possibly attempt to assist in a gentle and compassionate way.

Since I have never been a parent, I couldn't quite identify from that perspective. But then it hit me. A few days earlier, my wife Shelby and I were out running some errands. We had stopped at a store and I was going to run in for something. Shelby asked me something about getting a bite to eat while we were out, and I said something out of frustration, dismissing the idea as I got out of the car. As I got into the store I was struck by what had just happened. I saw Shelby's face and mood go from upbeat to defeated. I saw the smile disappear from her face. I almost started to cry when I replayed the scene in my head.

I thought to myself, "What have I done?" "How could I be so unfeeling?" "How many times have I done that and not realized it?" She was trying to be nice and I had just acted pissy. I basically reacted out of unconscious habit, which I've been doing most of my life, causing unnecessary suffering each time. This time I caught it and I felt the pain it caused. I got a glimpse of true compassion. When I got back to the car I apologized for my behavior and resumed the conversation I had so rudely cut off.

Once the memory of this came back to me at the DMV, I was able to look at the man and see myself in him. I have been just as abusive to my loved ones without knowing it (in the form of verbal spanking instead of physical). How could I condemn someone else for doing something I myself have done in one form or another? I then felt compassion for this man (who is me) hurting the one he loves most out of total unconsciousness. It makes me want to cry thinking back on it all.

In hindsight I can see clearly that we are all just trying to be good. But when we are punished for it, we shut down. It's a self defense mechanism to protect us from getting hurt again. We begin to put up barriers to prevent future pain, barriers which also cut us off from love.

I can look back and find countless ways in which I have hurt my loved ones, which can lead to deep feelings of guilt and shame. But guilt can be a teacher showing us that there is a better way. The better way is to become fully conscious of our habitual thoughts and transcend them. Be willing to drop the barriers we have put up, and find compassion for all of our fellow human beings.

Now, when I find myself judging someone else, I just take a quick look and see that I, too, have been just like that, felt just like that, acted just like that. I am no different from anyone else on this planet. I have no one left to judge but myself.

Chapter 50: Political Correctness

November 2, 2008

I hope you are enjoying this beautiful time of year. The Fall colors are in full force. The air is crisp. The insects that have been providing songs all Summer long are growing quiet. The nights are getting longer. But there is something else in the air. The impending election and financial crisis have a lot of people on edge. Politics seem to be on everyone's mind, and activists on both sides are doing their best to help ensure their candidate wins.

I have tried not to get sucked in by all of the drama, but I've watched a debate or two and listened to a few news stories. What I see is similar people who have different ideas about what is best for our country. What I also see is negative light being cast on those who have a different idea about what's best for our country. "I'm right," "No, I'm right," seems to be the easiest way to sum it all up.

Regardless of what our political views are, we think they are right, otherwise we would not cling to those views. When these beliefs are held too tightly, it results in negatively judging those who do not agree. Often times people will go to great extremes to prove they are right and the other person is wrong. This is what wars are fought over. In fact, the ego can't even entertain the possibility that our beliefs might be wrong.

The interesting thing about it is that no one can really be impartial or unbiased as long as they cling to beliefs. Everything they see and hear is colored by their beliefs. We only hear what we want to hear, which reinforces the belief that we are right. The spin doctor in the head (the ego) is being fed by the spin doctors of the candidates and the media (their egos).

I have not been very politically active since I found a new path to follow. If you haven't heard the story before, I had my first grand mal seizure, which led to my diagnosis, on November 7, 2004 (my anniversary is coming up). I had just learned that John Kerry had conceded the Presidential election before all of the votes in Florida had been counted. I was quite shocked, and as I went into the kitchen to tell my wife. I seized. A while later, in the ER, I was told I had a seizure.

Prior to that event, I was an avid Bush hater, and became very politically active after he lost the 2000 election. Most of what I wrote during the first term of George W. Bush's first term was political in nature, and I was becoming more and more consumed by it all during the run up to the 2004 election. Though I wasn't a big fan of John Kerry, I wanted to see Bush defeated (again). So this climactic experience ending in a grand mal seizure made me realize there is more to life than politics.

Needless to say, I am familiar with all of the frustration people have about politics. But I was lucky enough to have my priorities set straight after that Presidential election. I now see how harmful this animosity for opposing views can be to everyone involved. I may have my own ideas about who might be best suited to run the country for the next four years, but I see both candidates as people who want to win for what they perceive to be the greater good. I no longer have any animosity for anyone, and know that it's arrogant of me to think that I know what's best.

I thought I would leave you with some lyrics from a Michael Franti (of Spearhead) song entitled *"Is Love Enough"* that seems well suited for this occasion. May we all remain open to the possibility that our ideas about what's best may not be what is best after all.

We want freedom of speech
but we all talkin' at the same time
We say we want peace
but nobody wants to change their own mind
And So it goes on and on and on and on and on
for a thousand years
A thousand years I say
And it goes on and on and on and on and on
What language are your tears

are your Tears
Everybody wants to live the life of kings and queens
but nobody wants to stay and plow the fields
Everybody wants to tell their neighbors how to live
but nobody wants to listen to how they feel
And So it goes on and on and on and on and on
for a thousand years
A thousand years I say
And it goes on and on and on and on and on
What language are your tears
are your Tears
What I got to say right now
is love enough, yeah
love enough, yeah
love enough
or can you love some more...

Michael Franti

[As a post election note - I was overjoyed to see Obama win the election in a landslide. These are some truly historic times in which we are all living. I feel so lucky to be here to witness it.]

Chapter 51: And the Story Goes On

November 24, 2008

I almost called this one "That's My Story and I'm Sticking to It" but opted for something a bit simpler. Byron Katie likes to ask, *"Who would you be without your story?"* In fact, that's the name of her newest book. Eckhart Tolle also tells us that "You are not your story." I recommend spending some time looking at who you are without your story. Seeing yourself without your story involves completely dropping your past. If you set aside all of the ideas of who you are, who are you? Where are you? What are you doing here? What is all this?

It's a return to innocence we are talking about here. If you have observed children for any length of time, then you probably have vicariously witnessed what the world looks like to someone who has no preconceived notion of what it is they are looking at. The fascination with the world around them is present without the mental constructs and labels grownups have. It's joyful to watch an infant looking out at the world with a sense of awe. That's our true nature, but we lose sight of it along the way as we carve out identities for ourselves and for others.

"You are not your name." When that idea first came to me it was a bit shocking. It was as if the question, "Who would you be without your story?" was felt on a deeper level. I had been "Trey" looking at who "Trey" would be without his story. Then, all of the sudden, I had to take "Trey" out of the equation. If I'm not my name, who am I? Who is this "Trey" person without a label? We're so attached to our names because we have been called by them all of our lives, and we don't even realize that who we are is far more than just a name.

What was it before you knew what it was? Look at anything around you and ask yourself, "What was that before I knew what it was?" There was a time when you didn't know what it was. What was it then? It must have been a complete mystery. Just as the infant looks on the world with curiosity and wonder, you can see it with the same nameless sense of wonder that permeates everything we have come to know.

Throughout each day we are adding to and narrating our story. Our minds are story tellers weaving a tale about everything that pops up in our life. I'm constantly telling stories in my head. In fact, for each one of the blogs I actually write up and send out, I mentally write half a dozen others. My mind is busy writing instead of being still a great deal of the time. Or, it's caught in a vicious, repetitive, ego dominated conversation with someone who's not even there. When I realize it's happening I have a choice to either stop the story, or just notice that it's going on. But I still get sucked into my story over and over again.

Recently, I started compiling my past blog posts into one big journal. I've been writing these for the past few years and decided I would put them all together into a book. It was beneficial for me to go back and read what I had once written, but in the process of compiling them I realized that I was creating the story of the writer who shares these ideas, insights and teachings with others, still seeing myself as my own mind made identity (or the "little me" as some have called it).

Why not just stop telling my story? In my case, I think it's my mind's self-defense mechanism. When I am setting aside my story, dropping my thoughts, becoming present, connecting with the witnessing presence, becoming still, allowing everything to be as it is, etc., the mind tends to come in with an attempt to describe it or grasp it (it being presence, awareness, consciousness, etc.), thereby ensuring the mind's survival. It is attached to the story and doesn't want to let go. Who would I be without everything I hold true? It can be a bit scary to the mind, so it slyly starts seeking instead of resting in not knowing and the story is reborn. In fact, the story of the "little me" who can not see my true nature due to my attachment to my story is yet another layer to the story.

Raman Maharshi spoke directly to this issue when he said, "The only blockage to self realization is the idea that there is a blockage. You already are what you are seeking." Along those same lines, I think it was Papaji who once said, "Put your story away. It is not who you are. People usually live carrying a burden of past and future, a burden of their personal history, which they hope will fulfill itself in the future. It won't, so roll up that old scroll. Be done with it." Gangaji invites us not to deny the story, but not to indulge it either, and look to see what is untouched by the story.

I also like this quote by Byron Katie, "We do only three things in life: We sit, we stand, and we lie horizontal. That's about it. Everything else is a story." The story is sticky because we've been telling it for so long, but what we truly are is far more substantial than just a name or a history or a set of beliefs. Don't take my word for it though. See for yourself who you would be without a story. See what the things around you would be without a story.

Chapter 52: Let it Be

January 4, 2009

"Let everything be as it is." This is something repeated by Eckhart Tolle and is also referred to as "accepting what is," or accepting the "isness" of the present moment. I knew what it meant intellectually, and have been heeding this advice for a while now, but just recently experienced the meaning of the words more deeply. Despite the seeming redundant nature of this realization (based on previous experiences), I am slowly internalizing these pointers for what they are, due in part to continuous and repeated exposure.

In this particular case you'll have to bear with me on the mental imagery a bit. I was peeing in the toilet like I've done a million times before, and as I looked down, I dropped the story of what a toilet was, and looked at it from the present moment perspective, as if I had no past reference to tell me what a toilet was. I just let it be as it was. As I did so, the pure simplicity of its isness shined through. It had no name, no story, it was just present. I became simultaneously aware of the one looking at the toilet, and thoughts subsided. The toilet was still a toilet, but I just let it be completely as it was, in its natural state of nothingness, as in no name or description. It was simply a never seen before object. It was just a presence, or something here (yes, I was still able to pee without missing). The actions that followed involved closing the lid, flushing, washing my hands, etc., but those actions took place without my needing to "do" anything, and I was able to just enjoy witnessing each step happen.

It seems so simple to just let something be as it is, just by dropping the story and accepting what is present as an indescribable mystery, as no-thing. That's what, in essence, everything is. This experience also cleared up some confusion I had surrounding the word "essence." When used to describe a person in a phrase like, "Who you are in your essence," it used to conjure up the idea of some luminous core. But in simple terms, "essence" is just the simple, basic, fundamental existence of something (you might look it up in a dictionary).

A toilet is simply a molded ceramic object. But it becomes even more simple than that when viewed from a present moment perspective that doesn't know what ceramic is. It is, in essence, just some nameless thing with a certain shape and texture. But at the deepest level, when you are so present you have no past reference at all, it just is.

This slight shift in perspective is what it's all about. Take any object and look at it. Remove the idea you have in your head about what it is. Look at it as if you have never seen it before. What is it? If it has no name, no known purpose, no labels, what is it you are looking at? What is it, in essence (or on the most basic level), that you have in front of you? Let it be there, just as it is, nothing more, without trying to figure it out or describe it.

For me, what "it" is becomes much more clear. It takes on a richer texture, a new vividness, and an aliveness all its own. Then, it can't even be said to be an object, because what is an object? It just is. It is just as it is. Nothing more, nothing less. The innate beauty is available for viewing and experiencing when thoughts are removed from the equation. Thoughts about "it" cloud the simple isness of what it is. Its presence (or here-ness) is all there really is to it, but it is a wonderful thing to see.

Taking all of these terms and pointers in a more literal sense cleared things up for me. However, there appears to be varying depths of presence, this being a deeper experience than many I've had. I also have to say that becoming more fully present is still not easy for me to do very often. It takes a willingness, or one could say a determination, to see what is for what it is. The mind likes to step in and describe or instruct, but thoughts too can be viewed in this same simple way. They are present and can be viewed as "what is" in this moment, especially when you view them from the perspective of not being "your" thoughts, or not taking them personally. This creates some space between you (the witness of the thoughts) and your thoughts, which makes them less likely to suck you in. In short, you can change your perspective and change the world.

Chapter 53: Martin Luther King Day

January 19, 2009

I would like to wish you all a happy and joyous Martin Luther King day. The local NPR radio station played his "*I Have a Dream*" speech earlier, and I was moved to tears. The presence and passion that this man exuded shaped this country in ways one could only imagine at the time. His fearless fight for unity and justice through peaceful means served as an example of what life is truly about: Love.

Our nation has come so far in the last 40 years, due in great part to Dr. King and his connection with God. Now, his dream for this nation is taking a giant leap that could not have been imagined possible just a few decades earlier. Tomorrow, for the first time in history, an African American man will be appointed President of the United States of America. These are truly historic times.

This, too, is why we are all here. We are that change. We are that unity. We are that love. We are that fearlessness. We are that God. We are here to awaken to the truth of who we are, and bring about the same unimaginable change that will save the world, even if we have to die to do it.

In the meantime, feel that gratitude that has allowed us to be alive at this moment, to be present as witnesses to what love can do to change the world.

Chapter 54: Powerful Pointers

March 11, 2009

Since I discovered the idea of enlightenment a few years ago, I have been compelled to find out as much as I could about it. I have been a researcher of sorts, taking in all of these things, compiling them, sharing them with others, etc. My intellectual comprehension has continued to deepen, as has my experiential understanding. What I have found quite useful is reading things that resonate with me multiple times (this applies to listening to audio and watching videos as well). I have found that I am not always present enough to hear what is being said the first time. In effect, I may not be "ready" to hear something at one moment, and may be more receptive at another point. The other benefit to continuing to read about such things is that it serves as a constant reminder to look deeper. Otherwise, you read a book about enlightenment and say, "Well, that's interesting," and then leave it at that (which I strongly encourage you not to do).

It seems that we all want the same thing – a sense of peace that is not determined or affected by what the world throws at us. We all want to be happy, forever. So, in order for us to do that we have to be able to be completely at peace with who we are. How can we be happy when we are playing a role and trying to please others? Why can't we just be ourselves and not care about pleasing others? What if being ourselves is all it takes to please others? Then, we must first recognize who we truly are beyond the roles we have played all of our lives.

Along my personal journey, I have picked up various pointers that have resonated with me. Pointers are wonderful tools that help guide the mind toward what we truly are. We, in effect, use this mind to search for ourselves, but can't rely on it to understand what we are looking for. Intellectual understanding is great, and I think is a necessary part of finding your true Self, but eventually those mental concepts become a hindrance and have to be put aside to make room for the actual experience of what is true.

The pointers I have provided below have helped me experience understanding, rather than just the mental movement of understanding (though both seem to happen). I invite you to experiment with them on your own to see what happens. Try sitting with one pointer, or one sentence of a pointer for a while rather than just give it all a once over and forget about it. You may find that some of them "work" some of the time and not at others, but I recommend you try them all more than once. It might be helpful for you to copy and paste them into notes you place around as reminders.

Pointers:

When needless, repetitive thoughts arise and you notice them, turn them into gibberish or replace them with blah blah blah. Witness the thoughts as they turn into meaninglessness and disappear into silence. Keep bringing your attention back to this silence.

What's more real, the thoughts in my head, or the fact that I am here, now? Check in and see when you find yourself lost in compulsive thinking.

Simply look at yourself. Not in the mirror. Just look at what's animating your body. Ask yourself, "Who am I?" and follow your attention inward, as if your point of focus has rotated 180 degrees.

Look at who you think you are. Look at your mind made image of yourself, and how you think others see you. Are you creating a self image based on your projections of others? Aren't you the only one who sees that image of yourself?

Point your finger around at different objects, looking at what it points to along the way. Then point the finger at your own face. Direct your attention toward the empty space where you think your head is. Are you sure you have one? Check to see without looking in a mirror.

Who or what is looking through your eyes? Close your eyes and "look" (or focus your attention) at what's right behind your eyes. When you open your eyes, keep your attention on that space behind your eyes. Is that space what's aware of these words?

Focus your attention on your inner body. Feel the life energy underneath your skin. Feel your breath as it moves in and out. See if you can experience having a body with your eyes closed.

Be still and notice the stillness around you. Be silent and listen to the silence underneath the noises you hear.

Focus on the empty space around you. Look around and become aware of the space that encompasses everything.

Ponder this: Nothing ever happened. Everything in the past is just your imagination. Now is all that's real. Nothing outside of this moment exists without thought, and thought is just a complex neural network of synapses firing continuously in the brain.

There is just This. Just what is around you at this moment. The only thing that really exists is This. Right here, right now. Don't look for proof of the existence of other things, simply sit with the absoluteness of Just This.

Look at things for the first time, as if you have never seen them before. Drop your stories and labels and just look through the eyes that don't know anything. What was it before you knew what it was? How would a child see this?

Let it (anything) be just as it is. Look at the simple isness of it, and allow it to be as it is. See it only from the perspective that it exists. It is simply here, in your presence, and you are aware of it being present. That's all you can really be sure of, isn't it?

Look at your hands as they manipulate things. Watch them as they move around with their own innate intelligence. You don't need to control them, they know what they're doing. What will they do next? Just witness.

Ponder this: You are not the doer. See what it's like when you stop pretending to be in control. Just let the body lead the way and watch where it takes you. Watch the stories your mind creates about how unsafe it would be to give up control. Recognize that the mind's

149

reasons for wanting to be in control are based solely on speculation and not grounded in knowing. Smile at its lack of trust :)

I am ALWAYS right here. I am, and always have been, aware of my own existence, my here-ness, my presence. I am never not aware that I exist. In every circumstance, I am always aware of the space that I am in. The one constant, never changing fact is that I am aware of myself. I am totally conscious (aware) of being here (present) wherever I am. I still know that I exist even when I am unaware of my awareness. "I am" even when I don't consciously know that "I am."

Look at a past memory. What was it that was there witnessing it? What is here now witnessing it? What hasn't changed since then? What has always been here, wherever you have been, what ever you have done? What is that feeling of "you-ness" that has always been present at any given point in your life? What is that quiet space watching your life unfold? Just look at that without trying to find an answer.

What if this same witnessing presence that looks through your eyes is the same witnessing presence that is looking through everyone else's eyes? Look around at others as if your witnessing presence is actually the same presence looking through their eyes. In effect, take your awareness and wrap it around behind the eyes of others. The only difference is your outward appearance and your past experiences. You may have different thoughts, but that which is always here for us (our witnessing presence) is the same for all of us.

Driving (or walking) Meditation:

As you drive down the road (highways and byways where there is not stop and go traffic is best), focus your eyes a slight bit higher, or lower, or to the left or right, of where you would typically look. As you do so, open up your field of vision so that you are focusing not just on what is in front of you, but also what is in your peripheral vision. Expand your view so that you are taking in more of the scenery all around rather than just what is right in front of you.

Experiment by focusing at different points in front of you (i.e. a little to the left of center, a little above center, etc.). As you do so, remain aware of your peripheral vision. You can simultaneously be aware of what is in front of you and what is all around you. You can enjoy looking at the sky as you drive down the road just with a slight shift in your perspective. Even the lines painted on the road are more alive when they are noticed. Take it all in. Be aware of it.

As you do this, notice if you feel any tension in your body. Relax into it by taking a smiling breath. This is life. It's always all around you even when you don't notice, but it loves to be noticed. Don't be afraid to look around when you drive. You don't even have to turn your head to do it. Surrender to the fact that you don't have any control over your fate when you get in a car (or in any other circumstance for that matter). There's nothing to fear if life is giving you everything you need to experience in order to bring about your own fulfillment. You're not driving, you're being driven. Since we're all on a hunk of rock that's spinning a thousand miles per hour and hurtling through space at half a million miles per hour, why not sit back and enjoy the ride?

Chapter 55: Forgiveness and Gratitude

November 25, 2009

I hope you all are enjoying the change of the seasons. As the leaves fall, the sky gets larger, the nights grow longer. The stars seem brighter and more prevalent, and the outside world becomes more still as the birds and insects disappear. An exciting change is in the air.

Thanksgiving is also upon us. This is one of my favorite holidays because it serves as a reminder to look at all there is to be grateful for. I am grateful for my family and friends, for their love and support. I am grateful that I have come to see how much love there is in the simplest act. I am grateful for this beautiful planet we inhabit. I am grateful for technology that has enabled me to connect with so many people from my past and present.

At the most basic level, I am grateful that I exist. What a miraculous gift! How is it even possible to express enough gratitude for my pure existence? I am also grateful for all of the great teachings that have come into my life, which have led me to appreciate all there is with so much more intensity. Everywhere I look I can see things to be grateful for, if I look close enough. I would like to encourage all of you to look at all of the little things there are to be grateful for as well.

Many of us have mixed feelings about coming together with friends and family over the holidays. Some are eager to reunite, and some are a bit reluctant (or a combination of both). It can be a time of stress when it comes to preparations that need to be made. We want everything to be just right. We love it when things go our way. But things don't always go the way we want, which causes stress. I encourage you to recognize when this happens and be grateful that things are always going exactly the way they are supposed to, whether it coincides with our plans or not. Gratitude is the greatest stress reliever.

If the casserole gets burned, or the turkey gets overcooked, or someone forgets to bring dessert, be grateful. Things have gone exactly as they are supposed to and you've been given a great opportunity to realize and appreciate that. If disagreements happen among family members over politics or other family matters, another opportunity for growth has arisen. Once you realize that life could be no other way than it is right now, true forgiveness can occur. When we forgive, gratitude is a natural byproduct. This gratitude stems from not having to bear the heavy burden of resentment and anger. If we recognize that we are acting out of anger or frustration, we can then forgive ourselves and experience the gratitude of being forgiven.

As I was writing this, an Eckhart Tolle quote crossed my path.

> "Forgiveness happens naturally once you realize that your grievance serves no purpose except to strengthen a false sense of self (ego). Forgiveness is to offer no resistance to life – to allow life to live through you. The alternatives are pain and suffering, a greatly restricted flow of life energy, and in many cases physical disease."
>
> *The Power of Now*, By Eckhart Tolle (Page 136)

To truly forgive is to rid yourself of the burdensome weight of the past. Holding on to the past – whether that be 5 minutes ago or 5 years ago – will only lead to more suffering. To forgive and forget is to bring attention back to the only moment we will ever have: Now. Be thankful for Now by recognizing it as the one thing that matters.

Chapter 56: It All Starts With Mindfulness

December 26, 2009

I took a bit of a break from writing between March and November this year. I felt a need to wind down a bit. That's due in part to a feeling of, "What more is there to say?" Anything I said would just be a repeat of something that's already been said. But I have benefitted greatly from re-reading the same thing at a later date, as well as reading the same thing stated a different way. Plus, technically there is nothing "new" about anything I've said so far. So, I decided to start putting words on digital paper again and ended up at the beginning again – mindfulness.

If you want to live a better life, filled with less stress and anxiety, it's really quite simple. It all begins with mindfulness. The ability to notice what's going on in the mind and body is crucial, and also takes practice. We can't really control our thoughts because they have a mind of their own (no pun intended). What we can do is take a step back from our thoughts and witness their redundant, incessant, and often trivial activities.

Anyone can notice what thoughts they are thinking at any moment in time just by "looking." One way to start out might be to deliberately think thoughts, or mentally recite something while you watch the thoughts happen. There are your thoughts, and here you are, witnessing them. I recommend you do this as often as possible with your everyday thoughts since mindfulness creates a solid foundation for a better life.

You can really learn a lot about yourself when you watch how you think in different situations. I have found it immensely helpful to have read books by Eckhart Tolle and Byron Katie because they have helped point out specific repetitive thought structures that most of us have going all the time, as well as their adverse effect on our state of being. In fact, I probably wouldn't even know that these thoughts were going on, much less that they were at the root of my problems, had it not been for these great teachers. Simply knowing that thoughts prevent us from seeing the beauty all around is an idea that encourages us to get out of our heads and to wake up.

These are a few basic kernels of wisdom that I have found helpful to keep in mind while being mindful. – I am not my thoughts. – I can't control my thoughts, but I can observe them. – Thoughts only represent my past conditioning. – A feeling of worry means that I am mentally living in an imagined future. – When it comes to judgment, life is my mirror. – When I think negatively of another, it is actually only about me. – Forgive easily and forget quickly (this goes for yourself as well).

Mindfulness is a wonderful practice when applied to our interpersonal relationships. For example, if someone lashes out at me, rather than react I try to notice what thoughts or emotions are triggered. In most cases, no reaction is better than any action at all. I recognize that I am not the cause of their upset, nor they of mine. Past conditioning and mental stories are the actual culprits. When I do notice resentment, I bring myself back to the present moment, realizing that, in reality, the past never really happened. It's over. Only I can keep it alive by dwelling on it. If someone else decides to keep it alive, that's not my concern. However, I have found that when I let go of the past, it leads the way for the other to let go more easily.

Feelings of conflict or stress can serve as a reminder to notice what thoughts are doing to me. Since negativity always stems from some sort of judgment, it helps to mentally do The Work (by Byron Katie) throughout the day. Rather than go through all of the questions (Is it true? Can I know for sure it's true? How does that make me feel? Who would I be without that thought?), I typically skip straight to the turn around and look for truth in the opposite of my judgement.

The thing I've noticed about being mindful, and the knowledge I've gained from looking at my reactive nature, is that the movement of mind is very subtle. My ability to notice when I feel defensive has improved dramatically, and there is much less stress and conflict in my life. But, this can make it more disturbing when conflict does

155

occur. A feeling of frustration or disappointment is often present after a stressful moment has occurred. That feeling is like a hidden thought that is not in words but felt in the body, and is sometimes more difficult to notice. If investigated, I find that this negative feeling might stem from thoughts like: "I should know better," or "When will I realize that my thoughts are just a result of past conditioning?" or "Why can't I recognize that I am the only cause of conflict in my life?" or "When will I be free of compulsive thinking?"

All of these questions are simply forms of self-judgment that can carry us away into a story of lack and insufficiency if left unchecked. It helps me when I notice these thoughts or feelings of self-judgment to remember the necessity of all things. For example, it is necessary for me to feel or experience such thoughts in order to point out hidden pockets of resistance. It is my challenge to be made aware of my resistance to what is, then accept what is (even if I am accepting my own lack of acceptance). What I experience is what I need to experience, even if it doesn't feel all that pleasant. Accepting one's own failure to live up to some mind created standard is a practice that grows easier with continuous self-observation. As a result, failure is seen as success in spotting the falseness of the mind created standard.

In my experience, this is all part of a gradual Awakening. Life just gets better as we release old habits and ways of thinking. The past we drag around with us seems to get heavier as we go, but it has always been heavy. We are just starting to realize just how heavy it really is. Mindfulness is at the root of lightening the load.

Chapter 57: Why Ask Why?

January 31, 2010

Over the past few years I have been periodically describing my discoveries on the topic of enlightenment, or awakening, or self-realization, or whatever word turns you on the most. I have found that as I begin to see through the illusory nature of the world, and gain insights into the true nature of Being, I begin to mentally talk about it. The mental movement comes from the feeling that "This must be shared!" which is something I'm sure I've shared with you before.

This compulsion to share can be frustrating if looked at as a mental distraction that perpetuates the ego, or it can be seen as a gift in disguise. Something has been driving me to share these things. Mental notes to describe insights happen anyway, so why not just accept it and share them? They obviously want to be shared. Right?

On some level, this sharing has been my life's purpose for some time now. But in reality, I'm not really the one doing the sharing and they're not really my words. I am more like a pawn in the game of life being used to help other pawns realize their true nature. But that's easy to lose sight of when you are still grappling with ego, and so the story of being the separate doer continues.

Recently it occurred to me that my desire to share insights with others might actually be a veiled form of resistance, or a desire for things to be different from the way they are. My desire would be for "my" words to intensify "your" desire to awaken. "I" desire for "you" to be different from the way "you" are (i.e. more enlightened). However, by doing The Work on this idea it becomes obvious that it's actually "me" that I want to be different. After all, "you" are a mirror of what's going on in "me" and are reflecting my own non-acceptance of who I am.

From that perspective there seems to be two movements going on – there is the desire for you/me to be different, as well as a compulsion to share things that might make a difference. Which comes first? Is it possible that the sharing is always happening and that I am imposing the idea that it might be happening out of a desire for change? Or, do I want change so badly that I am driven to pass on pertinent information in hopes of bringing about that change? Are they really separate? Does it matter? Either way Life is living me and this mental dialogue is another way in which the mind likes to do what it does best – analyze the hell out of things.

I can spend my time trying to find answers, or I can spend my time trying to find the truth. The truth that can not be found by seeking. The truth that alleviates all need for answers. The truth that can't be put into words. It's the desireless state of full acceptance of what is. It's unconditional love. What's going on in our lives is exactly what needs to be going on in our lives. The life situation is an ongoing invitation for us to wake up out of the dream of being trapped inside a body. Acceptance and self-inquiry, not analysis, is key to self-realization. So, why ask why, when you can ask "Who am I?"

Chapter 58: A Dream Come True

February 6, 2010

Here is something I invite you to ponder. What if this moment was what you had been hoping and praying for all of your life? No matter what you are doing, whether it be taxes or walking the dog or reading a book or looking at a computer screen, imagine what it would be like if this moment was your dream come true. Don't get hung up on the skeptical thoughts, just feel what it feels like to have your hopes and prayers finally be answered. What does that feel like? Experience it fully and deeply – This is it! I finally made it! It's what I have always needed! Allow yourself to smile :-)

Pause to feel it........

I invite you do this periodically when you happen to think of it. For example, when you are feeling a bit bored or frustrated, stop and imagine that you have finally achieved your life's purpose. Sit with the feeling for a minute. This negative situation is actually what I have always wanted, but I decided to call it negative for some reason. This situation is the perfection I've been seeking all of my life. My life is now completely fulfilled.

Notice how the mind says, "Yes, but I don't want this. This is a lie." It may think what you're experiencing is painful, or wrong, or mundane, but what if your mind is actually what's wrong? See what happens if you ignore your doubts and concentrate on the feeling of, "Yes! This is what I have always wanted! My whole life has led up to this incredible moment!" Remember to smile and breathe a sigh of relief. Laugh if you feel like it :-D

Pause to feel it........

As you can see, that feeling you feel of fulfillment and joy and peace is actually available to you at anytime. What brings it about is not the situation, but the acceptance of the situation as being part of the necessary unraveling of your life situation. This peace sets in when you finally give up your desire to be at peace. You are always at peace, but you're too busy searching for it to notice.

When the seeking subsides, peace and joy can finally shine through. This is actually your true nature, and you can experience it every moment of everyday if you are open to it. All you have to do is realize that all of your dreams have come true, and are coming true every moment of every day. When all of your dreams come true, there is no more dream, only the truth. That's why it is called an awakening when you realize that you've already had everything you ever wanted. That's what Life wants for you. It wants you to be free. It wants you to realize the joy that you already are, and have always been.

Chapter 59: Spiritual Correctness

June 30, 2010

I have found myself at a bit of a crossroads lately. I've written quite a bit on the subject of enlightenment over the last several years, some of it representing where I envisioned readers to be on their own path, which has also reflected where I have been on mine. Up until recently, I have had somewhat of a "known" audience of about 90 people on an email list comprised of friends, family, and acquaintances, plus a blog that received very little traffic. So I have written with many of those people in mind. I have avoided using some terms and concepts that I thought might alienate those with only a mild curiosity, or those who still have firm beliefs. My hope has always been to open minds, so I have been mindful not to step on any sacred cows without watering down the teachings too much.

Joining Facebook has increased the exposure of my writing, and its circle of influence. The potential audience has now diversified and left me a bit uncertain as to who will be reading these words. Will it be spiritual adepts, teachers, critics, or will it be the curious and beginning seekers (I've heard from all of them by now)? Is it possible to write something that resonates with everyone? Whose needs am I trying to appeal to anyway?

There are online discussion groups popping up all over Facebook for truth seeking people. There are a lot of people out there, not unlike myself, who have a very firm grasp on the ideas surrounding awakening. They have it all figured out on an intellectual level, perhaps have had a few awakening experiences, and want to tell people how it is. I'm no different, but I am not one to debate another on what's true and what's not. However, that seems to be going on a great deal in some of these online discussion forums.

There are those people drawn to these discussion groups wanting more insights from fellow seekers or teachers. Often times these curious travelers just encounter the "know it alls" or "nit pickers" who disagree with everything and simply point out inconsistencies in what others have said. Some may have some useful pointers, but it would seem that there are so many "authorities" on the subject arguing that no one really knows who to believe. Ultimately, most of them are saying what's true for them and disagreeing with someone else who doesn't see things the same way. In many cases it's a philosophical debate over semantics among egos about Oneness.

After seeing this a couple of times, I decided these groups weren't for me. Obviously there is no harm in a friendly debate, which is what some of these tend to be, but if I don't resonate with what's being said on a deep level, then it's just brain candy and fodder for the ego. Having said that, I have benefitted from this ego fodder because it has pointed out my own judgments I have about people, but that's a whole other topic.

I have found some other online discussion forums that are a bit more "structured," which involve an actual teacher actively commenting or answering questions. A spiritual teacher who is willing to foster and facilitate online discussions is a wonderful thing. Not only is it enlightening, but it prevents endless debates from arising, and gently points readers toward what lies underneath the words.

As for my writings, there is nothing I can say that is actually true for everyone (except for maybe what I just said), simply because the truth can't really be adequately conveyed in words we can all agree upon (hence the never ending debates on Facebook). Some fault can be found in every statement, and I am finding myself acting on my own insecurities by being careful not to say something that a mind projected spiritual critic might take issue with. Basically, the ego is trying to protect itself from criticism by censoring what wants to be said. The increasing tendency to revise or keep quiet is how its desire for praise, and avoidance of conflict is being manifested.

This tendency of egoic protection is just another manifestation of how I have been living my life. My words and actions have largely been governed by what I think so-and-so will think (so-and-so is code for me disguised as another person). Now that I am becoming connected with more and more people via Facebook, I am noticing that tendency to second guess what I say more and more. I'm glad to be noticing that and feel compelled to share.

Now, I feel it's time to be a bit more free with my words, with less concern about how the imagined world perceives them or me. I can learn more about myself by seeing the "me" in "you" anyway. I think the key is not to make broad sweeping statements as an authority figure (i.e. "This is how it is."), but instead scatter ideas or questions that might spark interest. There is great potential here to reach hundreds of people who have settled with simply being content with life, rather than search for that unadulterated joy that's at their fingertips. That joy is what we are all searching for, and I want everyone to know that it is attainable at this very moment. This is something that I feel everyone should know.

Chapter 60: Trying to Make Sense of It All

September 12, 2010

For many of us, Autumn is approaching as the northern half of the planet begins to seemingly tilt away from the sun. The Fall Equinox is about a week away, and change is much more noticeable as days shorten, temperatures cool and leaves begin to fall. Change is constant, but one thing remains the same, and that reliable constancy is what most of us are all looking for in order to feel safe and secure.

I've written a bit about how we tend to go about finding that one constant truth a bit before, but this writing came out of a recent discussion regarding the analytical approach to truth seeking. Being a very analytical person myself, it was fairly easy to analyze the process of analysis ;)

Words at their very basic level are vibrations of the vocal chords to which we ascribe meaning. Each vibratory noise has a definition, typically one that has been agreed upon by those in a given society who speak a common language. If you believe in evolution, then it's safe to say that millions of years ago words began to form as a necessary part of human survival and development. As the human species began to migrate, so did different languages. I have no idea how the evolution of languages (much less dialects) really happened, but it would certainly be a fascinating area to explore.

An interesting thing about language is that most words not only have an accepted dictionary definition, but many are also accompanied by a mental image. That mental image usually varies from person to person, and is unique to his or her upbringing – cultural, parental, educational, etc. From that perspective it could be said that no two people see, read or hear anything the same way since everything we experience is filtered through, and interpreted by, our personal grasp of language.

For example, say the word "tree" and a mental image pops up of something, whether it is a generic tree or a specific tree, its setting is going to look different from the image that comes to mind for anyone else. The context of the conversation will also play a role in what that image looks like, and image doesn't have to be a picture at all. It could also be called a mental story. As far as I can tell, the same is true for most words (especially nouns) in our language.

So, what does this mean? It means that we are all seeing the world as one big run on definition, which we tend to assume is the same as everyone else's run on definition. Then, when we encounter someone who has a different definition of something, of course we think they are wrong. Why wouldn't we? After all, we have spent our entire lives determining which definitions are true and which aren't by using language to define the world and ourselves.

How did we determine what's true and what's not? How did we go about figuring out this whole ball of wax? I would suggest it's been through a process of reduction and deduction. Here are some definitions that will come in handy for the following discussion:

> Reduction - Latin - To lead back, or bring down the size, quantity, value or intensity of something
>
> Deduction - Latin - To move away from, or infer from a general principle

First, we reduce the Universe into manageable concepts. It seems too much to take in as it is, so we have to organize it using words and categories, which formulate the foundation of our beliefs about the world. Instead of seeing shapes and colors, we learn to see things as distinct objects with names and characteristics. This starts when we are very young as our parents introduce us to the world we inhabit, and it is absolutely necessary for our growth and survival.

As we reduce the world "out there" into digestible ideas, we use those ideas to learn more about how the world works, and how we fit into it. In order to do that, we make deductions based on a combination of our acquired concepts and experiences, which includes everything we have ever said, done, read, heard, seen, etc. We combine our definitions with our experiences, and use them to determine what the world is really about. It would seem we are hard wired to desire knowing the truth, even if it's only a relative truth.

Therefore, we reduce the whole into parts, then deduce or infer from our knowledge of those parts in an attempt to know the whole. So what happened to the whole that we had to reduce to find out what's true and what's not? We stripped it of its wholeness, then rebuilt it using words that someone handed us with attached definitions, which we assumed to be accurate. It's still whole, we're just not seeing it that way any more. We're stuck seeing our interpretations of it.

So, if our desire to know the truth is indeed instinctual, we go about trying to find the whole truth again with our filtered and diluted deductions about the world. We've broken it down, then built it back up, but we can never completely rebuild it. It's like a jigsaw puzzle of the Universe where pieces are missing – we are constantly running into gaps as we try to rebuild it.

When we run across an area where a piece is missing, we either fill it in by deduction (cutting a piece to fit), or just forget about it and leave it blank. But no matter how hard we try, we'll never get an accurate view by using what we've learned. That's why it's said that discovering the truth involves "unlearning" what we think we know, and a surrendering of our preconceived ideas, beliefs, and opinions.

Our ability to parse environmental data and extrapolate that information to reach certain conclusions about the inner workings of the world is a wonderful gift. The mind is a very powerful tool, and all you have to do is look around to see examples of how well it has served the evolution of the world we live in. All of the modern technology we take for granted (i.e. the wheel, indoor plumbing, electricity, atom bombs, iPads, etc.), we owe to the incredible power of the mind, but it's important to realize that it has an equally destructive side to it which has resulted in thousands of years of war, destruction and suffering. However, if you look you will see that most of the mind's energy is wasted on trivial matters, such as dwelling on past conversations, speculating on future encounters, wondering what others think of us, passing judgment, singing a song you can't get out of your head, etc. Here's a quote from Gina Lake's book, *Radical Happiness* (page 12).

> "We need the mind to function, but it is also full of useless and incorrect information – conditioning – that passes as facts. We need the aspect of the mind that allows us to do mental work, but we don't actually need the egoic mind to function. Self-realization entails a certain mastery of the mind that includes being aware of our thoughts and being able to discriminate between ones that have some truth and usefulness and ones that don't."
>
> Gina Lake

Finding the truth involves finding who we were before we "knew" everything. That's why the present moment is the key. Without past everything becomes new again, just like when we were infants looking at this world in a state of awe. Katie Davis says it well in her book, Awake Joy – "When you are free of past mental images, you recognize that the world is created new every moment that you become aware of it."

That new and mysterious world is staring you in the face 24 hours a day, and has been all along. Do you want to see it for what it truly is? You have to be willing to set aside everything you hold true. Drop all of your labels and look at what's in front of you right now.

Here's a parting quote from Eckhart Tolle's book, *Stillness Speaks* – "When you perceive without interpretation, you can then sense what it is that is perceiving. The most we can say in language is that there is a field of alert stillness in which the perception happens. Through "you," formless consciousness has become aware of itself."

Chapter 61: Inescapable Here

September 19, 2010

I've always been here.
Never to be anywhere else.
I can't get away from here.
I try to be somewhere else, but I'm still here.
I leave and yet here follows.
I'm momentarily lost. Where am I?
I'm still here I just wasn't looking.
I can't get out of here. I can't escape here. I'm eternally here.
I always thought I was going somewhere.
Now I know I'll never get there.

Here is the only place on earth, and everything happens here.
Where else would I want to be?
Where else could I be?
We're in the same here.
Together and here.
That's where we've always been.
You seem to be way over there, but you're still here.
Even when you're not around, you're still here.
My here, Your here, Our here, only One here.

Where is here?
Here is where I am laying in bed.
Later, here is at the market.
Then, here becomes an office.
Here seems to be changing constantly.
Here I'm sitting cross-legged, here I am standing, here I am walking.
Every moment here seems to be somewhere else, but here never
really changes.

A Seeker's Guide to Inner Peace

Here, present, now.
Nothing not here.
Just here.
Just this.
Only here.

Chapter 62: Your Body as an Antenna

October 23, 2010

Antennas are fascinating things. There are all of these invisible radio waves around us all of the time, going in every which direction, passing right through us. It's like we're swimming in them and have no idea. They are just waves until they are picked up by a seemingly innocent looking piece of metal. Those waves are then magically converted into beautiful sounds, and even colorful moving pictures (I am one of the few people that still use rabbit ears for my TV reception). Contemplating this magical happening led me to realize that humans are no different, which led to the creation of this meditation. In-joy :-)

[I recommend you pause (~) for a moment after reading each sentence]

Close your eyes and visualize your body as an antenna, picking up invisible waves of energy from the environment around you. ~ Feel the vibrational frequencies permeating your body. ~ Do you experience a tingling sensation? ~ Listen as your ears pick up sound waves coming in from all directions. ~ Feel those same sound waves entering your body as well. ~ Bask in the vibrations.

Feel the aliveness in your body as it breathes in air and expels it. ~ Feel the body where it touches the chair where you are sitting. ~ Stay with the sensations that are constantly being felt in the body. ~ Give your full attention to the bodily sensations.

Do you notice that the mind goes quiet as you do this? Many people say they wish there was an off switch for the mind. Well this is it. You can't give your full attention to your bodily senses and think at the same time.

Check back in with the sensations being received by the body. The head is the part of the body that receives the most sensations, like the top of an antenna. It hears, sees, smells, tastes, as well as feels.

Close your eyes again and check in with your head, the most sensitive part of the antenna. Listen to the sounds ~ Feel the face ~ "Look" at the empty space between your ears where the brain is located. ~ Do you feel the alive emptiness of your head? ~ It's quiet in there even as it takes in sounds.

Focus on that silent, empty space inside your head. ~ Focus on the silence underneath the sounds. ~ If thoughts interrupt this silence, focus your attention on the silence underneath the thoughts, and on the silence which exists before and after the thoughts. ~ Does this empty space in your head have any borders? ~ Keep your eyes closed and notice if that empty, silent space actually expands beyond your head. ~ It's all around the body, as well as within.

With your eyes open, look around and receive the visual input of the things around you. As you look around, wonder to yourself what it is that's looking through these eyes. ~ Look at the words on this page as if they are nothing more than shapes. ~ These black characters are being seen by something. What is that something? ~ Is it that same empty space behind your eyes? ~ Focus your attention on that space as you read the following, pausing at the end of each line:

Space is behind my eyes.
Emptiness is looking at these words.
Is this what I am?
These words are being experienced, rather than read.
They are being felt as they enter the body through my eyes.
One ~ word ~ at ~ a ~ time.
With eyes closed, experiencing continues.
There is only this.
Silent experiencing.

In-joy the peace that is available simply by paying attention to the experience you are having now, and by paying attention to that which is experiencing the now.

Chapter 63: The Miracle of Life

November 11, 2010

I am pleased to announce to the world that my wife Shelby and I are expecting. By that I mean that she's pregnant with our first child, who has an ETA of April 17, 2011. Needless to say, this a very exciting time for both of us. A miracle is unfolding as we speak :-)

To be honest, I never really had any interest in kids up until a year or two ago. Before that, I thought all of my friends were crazy for wanting them. I saw procreation as something that people were just programmed to do, and I didn't feel that same software running in me. But, as I started realizing that the secret to life's beauty and perfection lay in the eyes of innocence, I started paying more attention to children, especially infants, and how they view this world. That was the kindling that started the flame of interest.

When you look at a wide-eyed baby staring at everything around them for the first time ever, it can give you an appreciation for the miracle of being present only to this moment, in all its glory. They see everything without a story, without judgments. They are born free from preconceived notions and beliefs, and completely open to what life has to offer (that doesn't necessarily mean they like everything it has to offer). Infants have no fear of gaping at other people, or doing other things that adults tend to be embarrassed by, because they are ego-less beings. Babies are like little Buddhas, staring through untainted eyes, inviting us to do the same if we are willing.

As my appreciation for infants deepened, my desire to have a baby increased as well. It was like my biological clock had finally started ticking, and my wife and I started seriously talking about having a baby for the first time in our almost 20 year relationship. It was finally time.

Once the magic stick appeared with a pink plus sign, we were both very excited, but it didn't seem real until our first Doctor's appointment. That's when we got to see a little dancing being on the computer screen. Here was this tiny little organism that would one day be a human being.

That's when I started visualizing holding our child for the first time, staring into its all knowing eyes, while crying tears of joy at what a beautiful miracle this Life is. How magical it is to be able to create life. It's something I always took for granted until it dawned on me how magnificent it really is. Life has been giving birth to Life since the beginning of time, and I never really appreciated it until now. I now understand why they refer to babies as little Bundles of Joy, because that's exactly what they are. I tear up just thinking about seeing him or her smiling for the first time :-)

It may seem to go without saying, but everyone you see around you was a tiny, little being living in a woman's belly at one point (it's even crazier to consider that we were all tadpoles of potential before that). Each and every one of us emerged as little Bundles of Joy at one point. Imagine that! It's also important to acknowledge that every person that you meet is still that same innocent baby all dressed up in a mask.

We start weaving our identity masks at young ages, and have them well crafted by adulthood, but nothing underneath has really changed since the day we were born. If you really take a close look at a stranger or a loved one, you can still see the child in them, hiding under that mask. When you set aside your own mask, and look at the world through the eyes of the child you once were (and still are), you can see the innocence of others reflected back at you. It's almost as if our mask creates theirs.

I'm ready for little baby Boo (our nick name for him/her) to show me the way to unmasked Love, though it's hard to imagine not breaking down into tears of joy each time I look into those eyes. As you can probably tell, I am very excited about being a father (it still sounds kinda weird to say that), and I'm glad we waited until we were older to have a child because I needed to feel this sense of gratitude in order to be the best possible parent.

I could write for hours on this subject, but let me just end by saying, "Here's to the miracle we call Life and all the Love it has to bring." <3

Chapter 64: Stella's Life

January 8, 2011

My wife Shelby was admitted to the hospital on December 20th after she started feeling chest, back and arm pains. Since she was 23 weeks pregnant, we called the OB on call who confirmed that we needed to come to the hospital for some testing. She was diagnosed with HELLP Syndrome, where the blood platelet count drops and liver enzymes rise to dangerous levels. Two different OB/GYNs we had seen in the past confirmed that they needed to "take" the baby in order to save Mom. They also told us that our little girl was too small to survive outside of the womb. By now she was about 3 weeks behind where she should have been size wise and too small to be "viable."

We found out earlier in the pregnancy that she had a congenital heart defect, which was determined to be very operable with good chances of survival. We had also been told that she would most likely have Down Syndrome. Though all of that news was absolutely devastating at the time, we took things one day at a time, and gradually came to grips with the prognosis. Despite all of our worries about the future of our child, we were looking forward to welcoming her into this world with love and kisses.

On December 23rd at 5:43 p.m., Shelby gave birth to our baby girl, Stella Grace. But this didn't happen on its own. It took several days and different methods of induction to finally bring about contractions. Stella just didn't want to come, which made things that much more painful. The pain of dragging out the inevitable took its toll emotionally and physically. Shelby was subject to constant blood draws, blood pressure checks, and temperature monitoring. Her arms were black and blue from all of the needle sticks and IV ports. Since Shelby's health was stable, all we could do was wait.

When the time finally came, Stella came quickly. The doctor had just finished an exam, indicating that Shelby had finally dilated to 3 centimeters (they thought she needed to be at 5). The doctor and the nurse were on their way out when Shelby cried out that something was wrong. They seemed to think she was just having another contraction until her water broke and a little pair of legs poked out. As I stood there watching in a state of shock, the nurse and I helped her lay back. I held one of Shelby's legs and the nurse the other, while the doctor started assisting in the birth, and Shelby started pushing.

As I watched, I remained calm and kept reassuring Shelby that she was doing great and that everything was going just fine. In reality, I was scared of what was about to happen, but I knew deep down that it was going to be okay. I tried to convey that trust to Shelby by smiling as she kept pushing.

It was a breach birth in which the feet and body came out first, and the umbilical cord was wrapped around Stella's neck making her head a bit harder to come free. After some delicate coaxing, the doctor finally got the baby out. The doctor cut the cord, wrapped up the baby and put her in Shelby's arms. I knew our little girl was either already dead, or only had a short time to live, so we just started caressing her and talking to her.

The nurse listened with her stethoscope and told us that there was a heartbeat. We just stroked her, and cried, and smiled at each other as little Stella laid on Shelby's heart. She was tiny, only 9.8 ounces, but fully formed. She gasped for air a couple of times, which just broke our hearts more. We knew her lungs were not formed enough to actually breathe, which is why they told us there was no chance of survival. She moved her tiny little arms, once to grab Shelby's finger, and another time to put her own thumb in her mouth. She was too precious.

Our parents were all in the room and got to touch and talk to Stella as she laid on Shelby to keep warm. Another check of the heart by the nurse indicated the heartbeat was very faint. We cried and smiled and stroked her little head some more as the minutes ticked by. We took several pictures to capture the moment as best we could. Finally, at around 7:30 pm, she was pronounced dead.

At that point, we requested that they do the same thing they do with living infants, so they took her weight, measurements, and footprints. They dressed her in a dress we chose from their selection and took some more pictures. We finally decided enough was enough and they took her away. I have to say that the nursing staff was so wonderful. It made a very difficult situation much easier. These women put the "care" back in "Healthcare" and I admire their level of compassion.

It was an emotionally and physically exhausting experience for us all, but especially Shelby. She did so great. She was such a wonderful mother even though she had such a short time. She made sure Stella stayed warm as best she could, and made sure she felt loved as long as she could. I only wish it could have been longer.

Shelby was finally released from the hospital on Christmas morning. Leaving the maternity ward empty handed on Christmas was a tough thing to do to say the least. The walls were covered with pictures of beautiful little babies being held by adoring parents. It was as beautiful of a sight as it was painful.

So now we're learning to deal with the pain of a loss. Shelby's pain is understandably greater, since she was the vessel for this life. She loved being pregnant, feeling the tiny movements and kicks that I could never really feel. I do my best to comfort her and love her, though I can only imagine how deeply her heart aches to have Stella Grace back in her arms. Love was brought to life that day, if for no other reason, to show us that Love is eternal.

Gina Lake, a spiritual teacher and friend, had the following to say when she learned of our loss. I would like to thank her for her words of wisdom and reassurance. I would also like to thank all of the wonderful friends and family who offered their support during this trying time.

> "Recognize that the love you feel for Stella Grace resides within you and originates within you. She evoked this depth of love from you, and that is her gift to you. This love belongs to you and cannot be taken away from you, and it

will always be yours to give whether it is to her or some other child or to other people. She has shown you how deeply you can love, and that is a treasure. It may be her sole purpose in this life. That remains to be seen, but it is a worthy one.

It was not possible to avoid this challenge; it was given to you both, for whatever reason. It isn't for you to know why necessarily. You have to trust that it is serving a spiritual purpose. It is serving your soul's growth. All challenges hold a gift. Usually that gift is the spiritual strength and compassion that are developed as one learns to navigate such a devastating situation. The power you have is to either find the place within you that can be at peace and in love in even this situation or give way to bitterness, anger, resentment, and despair. This is the choice we are all faced with in any challenge. If anyone has a right to dark feelings, you do, but they serve no one and only keep you from your own beautiful Heart. What everyone needs now is to be in touch with the Heart." - email from Gina Lake

Chapter 65: The Underlying Should

July 12, 2011

My wife and I started attending a perinatal loss support group not long after we lost our daughter, Stella. It has been quite helpful to share our story with others and to hear what others have been through. I was amazed at how common infant loss really is, whether it's in the form of miscarriage or still birth or some other form of death before a child's first birthday. The statistics are quite humbling, and it's safe to say that you know someone, or know someone that knows someone, who has experienced a loss of this nature. People just don't talk about it, which is why support groups, both online and in person, are so helpful.

In one of our discussions at a recent support group meeting, we were talking about interpersonal relationships, and one of the men said that he didn't like to be "should on." When he felt like someone was telling him how he should feel, or what he should do, he would tell them, "Don't should on me!" I've known for some time that "should" was a word to watch out for, but I was glad to hear someone else acknowledge it.

"Should" is often used in a way that implies we know how things are supposed to be ("supposed to" is another way of saying "should"). This implies that we know how life "should" be unfolding in any given situation. We get upset or experience some form of frustration when we're wrong about things, which is why we never really allow ourselves to admit when we're wrong. Instead of accepting we're wrong, we declare our rightness by saying things "should" be different in order for them to be right, or at least meet our vision of what's right. So, you could say that no one is ever wrong about anything and that it's the world that's wrong, which explains a great deal about human conflict – both internal and external.

Though "should" usually comes from a place of "I know best," it doesn't always come across as negative. It can be as innocent as,

"You should try some of this pie," or some other type of invitation, or positive encouragement to join in something someone thinks you would enjoy. But it can be a slippery slope to more negative things if you decline an invitation but are continually pressured, or made to feel bad for declining. A slight shift can also turn an invitation into a suggestion with negative undertones, like, "You should really stop eating pie."

As you can see there is a gray area, and the person being "should upon" could easily feel like a victim regardless of the intentions of the person doing the "shoulding." However, most people are well-intentioned since they think they're right about everything. They are just innocently trying to make everything else right that they see wrong, or make everything the way it "should" be. Makes sense doesn't it? After all, that's what we've been doing all along – trying to make everything right in our eyes.

The bottom line is that the word "should" is usually at the root of all mental or emotional suffering. Look at any aspect of your life that makes you feel angry, sad, frustrated, etc., then look for the "should." When you feel a negative emotion, it typically means that something is wrong, as in something out there doesn't mesh with the way things are "supposed to" be.

The root "should" will take various forms. "He shouldn't have said that." "She should treat me better." "He should be more understanding." "I should have reacted differently." "I should be able to afford nicer things." In the context of our recent loss, the underlying should would be, "My baby should not have died." It all boils down to one central theme, "Things should be different than they are." The effects of a "should" range from mild frustration to deep sorrow, but you can always find a "should" where suffering is apparent.

How can I stop shoulding on myself and others? I can notice it. I can look for it when I feel upset and question it. Is it true that this or that should have happened or not happened? How did I get to be such an authority on what should or should not be? I can't possibly know the reason behind the things that happen in this world. I can second guess them to death and struggle to find answers to the question, "Why?" but it just leads to more suffering. I've found that it's much more helpful to recognize that "what is" could not be otherwise. Acceptance of "what is" is the only antidote for compulsive shoulding, and is also the key to peace. Acceptance is a way of saying, "Things are exactly as they should be, whether I can see any logic to it or not," even when "what is" hurts.

As a word of caution as you begin to notice the effect of "shoulds" in your life, be careful not to should on yourself for shoulding. In other words, don't think that you should be more accepting than you are. That just leads to circular frustration and is a form of not accepting your own habitual tendencies. Just notice when a "should" appears and look at it without judgment. Gradually the "shoulds" will become more apparent and cease to arise as much, or at least lose their power to cause suffering.

When it comes to relating to others, watch for "shoulding" on another "should-er." In other words, when someone else tells you what you should or should not be doing, and you say, "Don't should on me," it's another way of telling them what they should not be doing. By all means, feel free to call someone out if you feel so compelled, just notice that you are matching their "should" with your own. Another option in that situation is to notice that they are doing to you what you have been doing to yourself and others all of your life – acting out of a habitual tendency. When you notice their "should" without judgement or "counter-shoulding," conflicts (internal and external) quickly subside along with the negative feelings that typically arise when you are being "should upon."

You can't do this life thing wrong, but you can live with more peace when you get tired of suffering. So, consider this to be a polite invitation to see what it's like without "shoulds."

Chapter 66: Tis the Season to Be Jolly (or Not)

December 10, 2011

In preparing for the holidays, we've been putting up decorations, lights, a tree, etc. We didn't do much of this last year because of my wife's health and the pregnancy related complications leading up to Christmas, so it was important for us to get some of this done early this year. Shelby decided she wanted some outdoor ornaments (some lighted balls), which proved to be hard to find. We went to half a dozen stores looking for just the right thing, but we never found what she wanted and ended up buying the materials at a craft store that would come close to replicating it.

During this shopping excursion, which seemed to last many hours stretched over two days, I found myself being negative and feeling a bit put out by having to drive around town and browse stores during a busy holiday weekend. I was trying not to complain, but I felt like I had been taken over by this entity of unhappiness and couldn't snap out of it (often referred to by Eckhart Tolle as the pain body). I would periodically become aware of my unconsciousness, but it didn't do any good. In fact, noticing my unconscious behavior seemed to frustrate me even more. I was negatively judging myself for being negative, and the vicious cycle of judgment had begun.

There I was, the guy who likes to write about how perfect things are, and how all suffering is self-induced, etc., and yet I seemed stuck in a stereotypical male role of following my wife around a store with my hands in my pockets, feigning interest in things she pointed out, hoping that it would be over soon. The underlying disease came from a desire to be somewhere else, and the desire not to spend too much money on this project (a good example of how desire is at the root of all evil ;-). I could periodically see myself in that disgruntled role, implying that there was at least a glimmer of consciousness shining through, but not enough to break free of the spell.

When I checked in with my body, I noticed I was feeling fatigued and wondered if my physical state was contributing to my psychological state. Which came first? The physical dis-ease or the psychological manifestation of negativity? While I was looking for something to blame for my bad mood, I remembered a quote from *A Course in Miracles*, "I could be seeing Peace instead of this." I knew from past experience that this was true, but I couldn't see it in this particular circumstance.

I finally had a moment of clarity and remembered that acceptance of one's own resistance is necessary when you find yourself in a situation that seems unacceptable. I would usually associate this measure (of accepting one's inability to accept something) with a much more serious life situation, such as great suffering, illness, etc., rather than a trip to a busy shopping center, but to each his or her own.

Upon this re-realization, I reassured myself that it was completely okay for me to feel stressed, bitchy, etc. In effect, I forgave myself for my own non-acceptance (and for being a bit of a jerk). After that it felt like a weight had been lifted. I was able to relax a bit simply by being okay with my own resistance, and, interestingly enough, when you're okay with not being okay, everything feels okay :-)

This re-discovery of the power of acceptance didn't occur until near the end of our shopping excursion, and a nice scenic drive home helped round out what was an enlightening day of doing things that I didn't want to do, but had to be done. I share this with you, knowing that it may damage your opinion of me, in hopes that it may help you get through the holiday season in One Peace.

Chapter 67: Conclusion

I knew I wanted to compile a book out of my past writings a year or two ago, but felt like I really wasn't quite qualified enough. I'm not some enlightened spiritual teacher, so I had to wonder if my words were really worthy enough to be contained in a book to be read by people who might be looking for the secret to inner peace, etc. Isn't that like the blind leading the blind?

These limiting thoughts were delaying my decision to complete the book, in the hopes that one day I would be enlightened and be able to bring the book to a better climax, such as, "Then, it happened. My perspective shifted ever so slightly, and all became known. I realized that there are no individuals, and that we are all one. Part of a cosmic consciousness pretending to be human beings, etc." What a great ending that would have made, right?

It finally dawned on me that I was holding back out of fear of what projected "others" might think about some guy writing a book about enlightenment without being enlightened. Who would read that? Not me. My "time" is too valuable for that ;-) When I finally recognized and acknowledged that old program of insufficiency running interference, I decided to push forward. There will be plenty of critics, but I think there will be a larger number of people who get something from reading it (at least I hope so). I know I sure did when I went back to read all of my old posts again.

Anyway, once I decided to finalize the book, assembly and proofreading turned out to be fairly time consuming. But the challenge I'm facing at this moment is how to end this thing. I'm going to continue writing, and have already written a few other things to be posted later. Since there is no end in sight, how can I just abruptly say, "Okay, that's it for now. Stay tuned for the next one." No, I have to come up with a concluding chapter that does this book some justice. Or do I? Maybe I could just say, "Well, this seems like as good a stopping point as any. The End." That's sounding pretty good about now.

Maybe I could find a way that leaves people hanging on the edge of their seat in some way, like those season finales on TV that leave you going, "Those bastards! They can't just leave it like that!" That would be fun if it were that kind of book. Maybe my next book will be fiction and I can do just that. But where does fiction end and non-fiction begin?

Your life is like a work of fiction starring you, and it has all of the different plot twists, comedy, drama, and boringness that any movie that lasts for 80 plus years would have. We're all pretending to be stars in our own movie, which features all sorts of guest stars. If you're reading these words right now, then I've stopped in to be a guest star in your movie (Hi there!). When I go to the store, all of the other shoppers and check out clerk have become guest stars in my movie. But how much more fun would it be if you actually realized it was all just a movie? Then you could step out of it and enjoy it more fully. When you're trapped in it, the suffering of the main character seems so personal and yucky. Examine what if feels like to be the watcher of your life as it unfolds, instead of being identified with your character. It's just like any dream where you are actually all of the characters in the dream, instead of the lead actor.

Could it be true? Look around. Could this all be a dream? Could I actually be all of the characters in the dream and not know it? Has it all been scripted out since the day I was born, or is it being written and directed on the fly? Do I have any control over what's going to happen next, or is the only power I have to step out of the dream and wake up? Most, if not all, movies have a happy ending. What if this one does too? Can I finally relax and not sweat the small stuff? What if recognizing that there is a happy ending creates a happy ending that never ends? Wouldn't it be nice to live that happily ever after Now? Now is all there is, and that happy ending that never ends is concealed in that Now that never ends.

The End ;-)

PS

You are perfect! You are loved! You are here! What a glorious gift it is to be alive. Don't squander it pretending to be something smaller than you are. Wake Up!

Teacher Resources

I have included a list of some of the most helpful and influential spiritual teachers I've encountered below. They aren't really in any particular order, and it is by all means not inclusive. There are many more teachers that I have encountered only briefly, but whose words have been helpful.

Byron Katie - What can you say about Katie? All I can say is read one of her books and see for yourself. Some may call her a self help guru, but she is just a beacon in the night inviting people to question their beliefs. "*A Thousand Names for Joy*" is hands down one of my favorite books, but her other books are great too.

http://www.thework.com
http://www.byronkatie.com

Eckhart Tolle - Eckhart is probably one of the most well known spiritual teachers in the Western world. His teachings have touched tens of thousands of people, and that circle of influence continues to spread. I think the reason for his popularity is that his pointers are simple and resonate with people on a very basic level. Just a glimpse of what life in the present moment is like is enough for people to want more presence in their life.

http://www.eckharttolle.com

Adyashanti - I've enjoyed several of Adya's books (i.e. "*Emptiness Dancing*," "*The Impact of Awakening*," etc.), but his website has a great deal of free audio and essays as well. I highly recommend checking him out.

http://www.adyashanti.org

Gangaji - For me, Gangaji rounds out the top four of the most well renowned Western spiritual teachers. I enjoyed her books, "*A*

Diamond in Your Pocket" and *"You Are That,"* as well as many of the writings and videos I found on her website and You Tube.

http://www.gangaji.org

John Sherman - John was one of Gangaji's students when he was serving time in prison (her prison outreach program has helped a number of people). All of his teachings are free through his website in the form of eBooks and webcasts. His message is as simple as the nose on your face – just look at yourself (figuratively). He has several websites that I recommend you check out. I also invite you to join the Just One Look email list to become a part of the inward looking movement.

http://www.justonelook.org
http://www.riverganga.org
http://www.thefearoflife.org
http://www.lookatyourself.org
http://www.johnsherman.org
http://www.silentheart.net

Katie Davis - One of my other favorite books is, *"Awake Joy: The Essence of Enlightenment,"* by Katie Davis. Her teaching approach is from the heart and points us back to who we are in our essence. She makes herself very available to people interested in awakening. I highly recommend you check out her website and blog, as well as the free videos she has to offer. Her husband, Sundance Burke, is also a spiritual teacher you might enjoy.

http://www.katiedavis.org
http://www.awakebykatie.blogspot.com

Gina Lake - Gina has written numerous wonderful books, and has a great deal of audio, video, and excerpts on her website. Her teaching is like a combination of Eckhart Tolle and Byron Katie, which is probably why I resonate with it. She is also very approachable for people with questions.

http://www.radicalhappiness.com

Nirmala - Gina Lake's husband, Nirmala, is also a spiritual teacher. His teachings point us back to the direct experience of Being in a direct, no nonsense way. I recommend you check out his website as well.

http://www.endless-satsang.com

Jeannie Zandi - I had my first real heart opening experience during my first satsang with Jeannie. Her message is one of Love, Beauty and Surrender. Truly a lovely human being.

http://www.jeanniezandi.com

Norio Xoximei Kushi - Norio is a truck driver by trade, who experienced an awakening while driving cross country. He points out beautifully how language is the root of our confusion, and how tangled up in words we've become.

http://www.demystifyenlightenment.org

Scott Kiloby - Scott has a simple approach as well. He writes about overcoming suffering and addiction, as well as stepping out of the story we have mistaken ourselves to be.

http://www.kiloby.com

Karen Richards - Karen is a wonderful young woman with a very large heart. Her invitation to investigate the nature of reality resonates with a vast number of people, and I recommend you check her out on her website and on Facebook.

http://karen-richards.com

Karen McPhee - I highly recommend you check out the free guided meditations on Karen's website. She was one of Eckhart's students turned teacher, and has a very nice way of pointing people toward the present moment.

http://www.livingnow.ca

Pamela Wilson - In listening to some audio of Pamela, I realized that loving the ego was actually more important than trying to get rid of it. She teaches us to embrace all of our so-called negative sides, and get curious about it all.

http://www.pamelasatsang.com

Catherine Ingram - The thing I remember most about reading Catherine's book "*Passionate Presence*" is the quote, "Just this." It gave me a new felt understanding of what presences is all about.

http://www.dharmadialogues.org

Bentinho Massaro - Bentinho is a very young man with a great deal of joy that he exudes in the rapidly growing number of videos he's putting out there. Check out his website as well as You Tube.

http://www.free-awareness.com

Benjamin Smythe - His message is simple, "You're Perfect." He has a great sense of humor about everything and is very reassuring about the fact that you can't do this life thing wrong. Check out his quotes and videos.

http://www.benjamintsmythe.com

Rupert Spira - Rupert uses the direct approach of experiencing what's here, now. He has a lot of questions answered on his website, as well as video inteviews.

http://non-duality.rupertspira.com/page.aspx

Though there are a whole host of teachers out of India, my studies have been with mostly Western teachers and I am only familiar with a few from the East. I can safely say that the words of the following teachers have been of great use to me. They are also some of the most well-known sages of the 20th century. They have all passed away now, but all of them have left behind a legacy that will continue to influence many generations to come. I've included some web sites to use as starting points, which have links to countless other sites out there for each. I'm sure you will find some powerful quotes that will resonate with you.

Ramana Maharshi - The Father of Self Inquiry himself. All paths lead here. "Who am I?"

http://www.nonduality.com/ramana.htm

Nisargadatta Maharaj - The original stand as Awareness man. "I Am That."

http://www.nonduality.com/nisarga.htm

HWL Poonja (Papaji) - Known for saying, "Call off the search. Stop. Be still."

http://www.avadhuta.com

David Hawkins - I owe David a big thank you for the guidance I needed when I first started looking for answers to life's big questions. His book, "*Power vs. Force*" was the first book I read on enlightenment, and it really cracked open my mind. I was hooked, and read all seven of his books (he has written more since then). I also joined a Hawkins discussion group, met lots of great people, and eventually found all of these other great teachers. I drifted away from his teachings after discovering Tolle, and never really looked back. One of the faults I found in David's teaching was that he made it seem as if obtaining enlightenment was damn near impossible (and very painful). It also seemed to me like David's writing was becoming more unnecessarily political, which is when I knew I had gotten all I could get out of his teachings.

http://www.veritaspub.com

There are several other websites that serve as reliable resources for people wanting to find out more about different teachers. Though this isn't an all inclusive list, I am familiar enough with these sites to recommend them. Just like any other search, one page leads to another, and another, and you always find just what you need at just the right time.

Satsang Teachers - I have to recommend this website because it led me to discover several lesser known teachers that I probably never would have found otherwise. There are a rapidly growing number of teachers out there, and this site is designed to be a calendar listing for all of the ones that are currently active. I can't vouch for all of the ones listed, but I know at least a dozen of them from personal experience and am reassured that they are doing some sort of screening before listing them.

http://www.satsangteachers.com

Here are a few other sites of interest. If you have more teachers to recommend or resources you would like to share with others, feel free to write a reply comment to this blog post.

http://www.nonduality.com
http://www.stillnessspeaks.com
http://www.nevernothere.com

Appendix

Article from *Spirit in the Smokies*, April 2006
From Epilepsy to Enlightenment
by Trey Carland

My life changed tremendously when I had a grand mal seizure on November 7, 2004. For about a year prior, I had been having what I affectionately called 'revelation spells.' These lasted a minute or two and I felt like I was having some sort of divine revelation and suddenly understood everything in a whole new light. Along with this euphoric feeling was the loss of control over the thoughts in my mind. I became the observer of my thoughts; sort of like being the observer in a dream.

Try as I might, I could never remember what my mind had thought during those times. I could observe, make mental notes on what it was thinking, then quickly forget. It was frustrating, but a pleasant feeling none the less. As it turns out, those brief episodes are called complex partial seizures.

After the big one hit, I was diagnosed with epilepsy. This term fits anyone who has had more than one seizure, so it didn't answer any questions. None of the tests I had, nor doctors I saw, answered my burning question of, "Why?" The only thing I learned was that the seizures were originating from my left temporal lobe.

Looking for Root Causes

I have always been an analytical and intelligent person, earning three masters degrees in different areas of business, with an ability to find the most efficient way to accomplish a task. This is handy in my work of helping to run the family business, much of it on the computer. Before all this happened, I led a fairly average American life in that I drank, smoked, watched a lot of TV, and ate predominantly processed foods.

My only hobby was working outside in the yard with my wife and our dogs. I rarely read for pleasure and had all but lost touch with my youthful desires to change the world, though I was beginning to get sucked into the political dramas of our world society. Yet I did have a growing sense that everything happens for a reason, and was determined to find the reasons for my disorder.

I found myself unhappy about being dependent on a mind-altering pharmaceutical, the anti-seizure medications, for the rest of my life, so tried to wean myself off them. I had more grand mal seizures, which are quite unpleasant, so I reluctantly chose to take the drugs, finding one with the least amount of side effects.

My wife and I began researching epilepsy, coming up with several possibilities—from aspartame to mercury—but none seemed the clear, defining cause. I began seeking out alternatives, seeing an MD who was also an Oriental Medical Doctor, taking several herbal supplements, changing my diet, and seeing a counselor due to the moodiness side effect of medication. This dramatically opened my horizons of perception and self awareness.

I read about famous people with this disorder, looking for commonalities, and learned of an interesting link with shamans. I researched religion and spirituality, all of which was interesting but I wanted, needed, to know more.

Acknowledging Universal Consciousness

From a meditation class offered at Lotus Lodge, which is near my home, I explored the Buddhist practice of letting go inhibitions and putting thoughts on hold temporarily. This left me with a "warm and tingly" feeling, eager to learn more. I began reading about quantum physics, about the spiritual and psychological aspects of life, illuminating ever more about myself and the world around me.

Several months ago, my wife and I began taking a shamanic dreaming class. One of our first homework assignments involved dreaming for a classmate on a specific question they wanted answered. The results were stunning. Each of us actually had relevant information about the answer to a total stranger's burning question!

Magically, this was at the same time I was reading David Hawkins' book, *Power vs. Force*, which explains how we are all part of universal consciousness and how to tap into it using kinesiology. Reading about it while experiencing it firsthand changed the way I view the world.

It was then I realized that I had been given the gift of seizures in order to discover all that I was missing. In that moment I changed my course from finding the cause or cure for seizures to knowing that I was on a search for enlightenment.

As for the seizures, I have been reluctant to part with them. Rather than continuing to up my medication until the seizures went away, which is what my doctors have recommended for the last year, I have it regulated so that I no longer have grand mal seizures but continue to have partials about once a month. This seemed the only way to measure the impact of the alternative treatments.

Rather than euphoria, however, as in the pre-diagnosis days, the partial seizures now come with an aura of anxiety. This is partly due to fear that it might be a big one, yet I still think there is something to learn from this experience. These strange "dreams" might hold some key to higher levels of awareness.

Thankfully, I am leading a much healthier life than before. I've given up TV, read for pleasure whenever possible, try to practice mindfulness in everything I do, and am much more conscious about what I eat and drink. I have also been doing non-dominant hand writing/drawing in an attempt to explore unused portions of my brain.

My desire to do what I can to make this world a better place, through nonpolitical means, has been rekindled. In short, I feel one step closer to where I never realized I needed to be, and I owe it all to something I never wanted to have, but now want to keep as a possible means to where I want to go. Ain't life strange?

Notes to Self

About the Author

Trey was born in Asheville, North Carolina, in 1973, and he still lives and works near Asheville. After dropping out of high school at the age of 16, he went on to graduate from Western Carolina University, in Cullowhee, NC, with a bachelor's degree in Computer Information Systems at the age of 19, and completed the Master of Business Administration degree two years later at the age of 21. He and his now wife, Shelby, decided to take a Master's in Human Resource Development after that, while they were deciding what to do next. Later on he completed the Master of Entrepreneurship degree program, because his parents had created the program and he thought it sounded like fun.

He started his first venture, a web page development company, at the age of 18. After completing his MBA, Trey spent some time as a business plan consultant, working for business owners looking for venture capital funding. He now runs the family business, an academic conferencing and publishing company, and oversees the production of seventeen academic journals.

When Trey was diagnosed with Epilepsy in 2004 at the age of 31, he started trying to make sense of a world that he thought he already knew. His research took him well beyond the realm of business to a study of science and medicine, including everything from biology to physics to alternative healing practices.

Looking to fill in the gaps in what these subjects were missing, he began studying various religions, shamanism, metaphysics, spirituality, meditation, and eventually discovered advaita and the idea of cosmic consciousness. He then realized that enlightenment and self-realization was what he had been trying to find all along.

Trey is the co-founder of the Asheville Sangha online community (www.AshevilleSangha.com), which was developed for people interested in non-duality, self-realization, meditation, enlightenment, etc. He also facilitates Awakening Practices Group meetings in the Asheville area. Trey invites contact and exchange with any reader who feels a draw or a need. You can reach him, and follow his current writings through his on-going blog, or Facebook:

http://compassion-blog.blogspot.com

http://www.facebook.com/trey.carland

www.ingramcontent.com/pod-product-compliance
Lightning Source LLC
Chambersburg PA
CBHW060251290526
45789CB00001B/280